RESILIENCE

RESILIENCE

RESILIENZA

The Capacity To Persevere, Adapt And Survive

(La Capacita di Perseverare, Adattare e Sopravvivere)

Stories about the people of Serrastretta, Calabria, Italy
and how resilience has shaped their character

by
Chris Bevevino

REGENT PRESS
Berkeley, CA
USA

Printed in the U.S.A.
REGENT PRESS
Berkeley,California
wwwregentpress.net

TABLE OF CONTENTS

(Note: The text of the book contains photo references. A reference will appear (P1) and refer to the Photo Gallery with all photos in numerical order)

Map of Italy
Map of Calabria
Portrait of Leonardo da Vinci (by the author)
Portrait of Rosario Bevevino (by the author)
Who Was Dalida?
Verses (written by the author in contemplation of this book)

DEDICATION
(Dedicazione)

This book is dedicated to the millions of Europeans who came to America between 1880 and 1920 to seek a new and better life; and in the process turned the United States of America into the greatest country in the world. Because of their resilience, their perseverance, adaptability and survival skills perfected over centuries, they played a major role in the USA's development and attained a success never previously achieved in multicultural experiments dating back thousands of years. As you will see, the best model came out of Sicily in the 12th century. These characteristics of resilience are particularly true of Italians, those from Sicily and Calabria. I am proud to be one of their descendants.

— The Author

INTRODUCTION
(Introduzioni)

"Nature's gifts are simple and direct,
nothing is wasted or superfluous."
—Leonardo da Vinci

I am in Italy. I woke up this morning here in Lamezia Terme, Calabria and laid in bed staring up wondering if I would get showered by termite dust from the old wood beamed ceiling above. "Why worry about that?" I said, when I also kept asking myself, "What am I doing here?" Over and over, probably 100 times I asked; and since I was the only one with the answer, I reiterated to myself that the purpose of my journey, and the reason for writing this book, was to find the answer to a nagging question.

Why were the European immigrants who came to America from Italy, and other western civilization countries, so resilient? The answer, I believed, is found in the simplicity of their value systems, their reliance on nature, their faith in God, and their strong family bonds. So here I am embarking on my investigation; but then I recoiled in fear that the answer may be a different one.

Surely Leonardo da Vinci could not have been wrong when he wrote "Nature's gifts are simple and direct, nothing is wasted or superfluous." After all, he relied on nature as his authority, rather than those men of letters, learned classical scholars who came before him. This great genius could not have gotten it wrong. And I witnessed in my own grandparents, born in Serrastretta just a few kilometers away, a strength and resilience unsurpassed. To them, nature was their bounty. Sicilians and Calabrians understood this concept before da Vinci wrote those words. As Americans, we look to our European ancestors with pride, or at least most of us do. Our past is our present and our inheritance; and right or wrong, good or bad, it has shaped us. We cannot disown it and refuse to be identified by it; better to embrace it as who we are.

Finally rising out of bed that morning, I fully realized what was ahead of me and about to begin; yet I am still hampered by a lack of fluency in Italian. As the weeks and months go by, I will become more comfortable with the language with the support and coaching of some wonderful associates.

You will read in this book some remarkable stories of Calabrians today in Serrastretta and its surrounding villages. Serrastretta was founded in the 13th century by five Sicilian Jewish families escaping persecution by the Inquisition. They fled Sicily and went to a remote area of the foot of the boot. The five family names are Bruni, Fazio, Mancuso, Scalise, and Talarico. My grandmother from Serrastretta (the village of Angoli) was a Scalise. Serrastretta is surrounded by 10 smaller villages, all incorporated into its municipality. The five major satellite villages are Accaria, Angoli, Cancello, Migliuso and San Michele. Descendants of these five families are still there today, and I wanted to learn from them, first hand, the ingredients of their resiliency, just what it is that allowed them to survive (and even at times thrive) through centuries of hardship, turmoil, starvation, political upheaval and required sacrifices that Americans today cannot even comprehend. Nature was their bounty, even at times when it did not provide enough. Through it all, they have emerged warm, friendly, happy, content, and without anxiety.

I listened to their stories, delved into their value systems with searching questions, and examined their relationship with nature and their surroundings. They understand, as da Vinci did, about nature's authority, directness and simplicity. Their beliefs and their true-life stories convince me more than ever that man, as a part of the natural order of things, is in fact nature itself. The further man moves away from nature, the less human he becomes.

The descendants of those five Sicilian families represent a true blending of both ancient and the Judeo-Christian value cultures, the reliance on nature and what the earth provides, and respect for procreation and the family unit. Most of these people became Christian Catholics out of necessity; and one might say a positive effect contributing to their resilience.

So...we will examine "resilience." What is it? Where does it come from? Is it inbred and self-sustaining? Can it be lost and rediscovered? Was the emigration of Europeans to America in the late 19th and early 20th century a prime example of resilience? The answers to these questions can be found in the words and stories of the Calabrians featured in this book; and when you listen to them, you begin to understand why our European ancestors possessed a greatness born out of simple values that in a brief span of time literally swept the United States of America to world leadership. Combined with a strong democratic governance and the bounty of our land, already here waiting for them, and the results were inevitable.

It is somewhat of an irony that one of the very first Serrastretta residents I interviewed and write about in this book is a woman born in Pittsburgh, Pennsylvania who has since moved to Calabria where her grandparents and parents were born. She is Rabbi Barbara Aiello, the first female Jewish rabbi in Italy who now has her own synagogue in Serrastretta. She is today considered the leading authority on the Jewish roots of people in Calabria, and she estimates that 40 percent of all Calabrians have Jewish ancestors coming there from Sicily, Spain, Portugal and elsewhere to escape persecution from the Inquisition.

There are so many people in the greater Serrastretta area with the same last name it becomes very confusing to keep track of just who is who. Some of the most common surnames are, of course, the founding families of Bruni. Fazio, Mancuso, Scalise and Talarico. But other very common names include Lucia, Gallo, de Santis, Aiello, Mazzei, Iuliano, Cianflone, Maruca, Gigliotti, and Molinaro. Some other local surnames I noticed at the cemetery included Bellina, Fiorentino, Morelli and Rossi. Most women are referred to by their first name and maiden name, but ironically, in some cases their maiden name and married name could be the same.

In this book you will meet some remarkable people:

the young and the old, laborers and professionals, business owners and consultants, clerics, professors and educators, students, farmers and artisans, the rich and the poor. The many people, more than 100, that I spoke with not only come from Serrastretta and the villages within its comune, but also from other nearby villages such as Amato, Decollatura, Cosensa, Miglierina, Pianopoli and Tiriolo. Depending on how rich and poor are defined, you will discover that everyone is wealthy because Calabrians believe life is a celebration. They will give testimony to the lasting resilience of Calabrians and their ability to persevere, adapt and survive. "La capacita di perseverare, adattare e sopravvivere."

Patience is a necessary virtue for Calabrians, because nothing in Calabria happens fast or on time. If it is true that time heals all wounds, then Calabrians are its master. And they never seem to panic under the worst of circumstances. If your ancestors were from Calabria (or Sicily), you will thoroughly enjoy reading this book. It will not only help with your understanding of who they were, but also who you are. It is a boost for your self-esteem and your pride; and hopefully, it will make you a better citizen of your home country. The reader should understand this book is written primarily for English speaking audiences; and I have also expressed certain of my personal opinions, all based on first-hand observations.

In some ways, the successful completion of this project, whether the book gets published or not, represents for me a redemption of the past; things I would like to have a second chance at doing better. Call them mistakes, or scars that I wear; and even though fully healed, some anguish remains. The book is a gift to me and to the reader. I hope it is enjoyed and that the reader takes something from it. When I finished it, I was able to walk away knowing I gave it my best; and when I turn to look in the mirror one last time, I will be comfortable with the reflection.

Join me in this love affair which I call the "Il romanticism della vita in Calabria."

I invite you to share in the discovery of the characteristics that are the source of the Calabrian people's resilience; and I will conclude this introduction with a verse I wrote when contemplating this book. It is titled "Our Inheritance."

OUR INHERITANCE

Solace comes from the knowledge and
Understanding of one's heritage and roots.
In a nation whose people come from
So many other places, the mystery of
Our beginnings to often remain so.
The stories told are small bits and pieces;
And what is passed down is incomplete,
What is known we treasure and keep.

A college classmate and I had a warm
Heart-felt conversation recently about
Our common Southern Italian heritage;
And the forces inside compelling us to
Unravel who we are, from where we came.
Our pride urges us to identify with the
Blood of old, those long gone, and record
What we can for generations to come.

If one has faith in what's just been said,
It begs the question that must be asked.
Why are we not at peace with what our
New World forefathers created for us?
The answer lives in our naïve youthfulness,
Too short a history since the union formed.
The fear not knowing how long it will last.
What can we discern from ancestors past?

Look to forebears, those many years gone,
Trying to understand how they survived.
We are the heirs of their Western World;

Are in such awe of what preceded us.
From the Steps to the Channel and beyond,
From the Boot to the Nordic, sending sons.
We are their legacy from centuries past,
Only to wonder how we make it all last.

Examples are many, just test one or two;
Travel back to the shores they left,
Observe their comfort, their peace of mind
That exists within our ethnic kin, and
Unlike us, their ageless past is present.
They embrace from where they came,
And accept full ownership, with pride,
In the greatness of their ancient past.

They are comfortable with who they are.
We, by contrast, cannot be the same;
But there is value in what we leave behind.
As the years pass by, the search carries on
To understand how we came to be.
Our greatest achievements still yet to come,
Knowing full well we can make no claim,
For we have not yet suffered their pain.

CHAPTER I:

The Evolution Of Sicily And The Foot Of The Italian Peninsula

(L'Evoluzione Della Sicilia E I Piedi Della Penisola Italiano)

"Although we have no reliable figures, such evidence as can be garnered suggests that general literacy in Sicily under the Byzantine Greeks was higher than in most of Europe and that it increased further under the Arabs."

THE PEOPLE OF SICILY, A Multicultural Legacy
By Louis Mendola and Jacqueline Alio

It is easy to imagine that the island of Sicily and the southern-most portion of the Italian peninsula have always been inhabited by humans; at least since the volcanos that created these land masses cooled. And even if there were inhabitants there from the very earliest years, who is to say that these people were not wiped out by new volcanic eruptions? What we do know is that evidence suggests these lands were inhabited at least as far back as 9,000 to 10,000 BC.

According to Sandra Benjamin, author of a well-researched book titled "SICILY, Three Thousand Years Of Human History," the island's history only goes back as far as the beginning of the written word there. She says, "History is written record; the story of Sicily's colonization is prehistoric." Lewis Mendola and Jacqueline Alio in their book "The Peoples of Sicily, A Multicultural Legacy" expressed it this way: "'History is written by the victors'" only when they have a written language." With this thought in mind, the first peoples to inhabit Sicily did not possess the communication skills of an alphabet and the written word. What is known of them is based on what they left behind, their artifacts and ruins. But, we known these inhabitants were there, and what they left gives us clues about who they were and where they came from.

Who are Sicilians? The answer to this question is so complex that an argument could be made there are no true Sicilians. This long inhabited strategically placed island in the middle of the Mediterranean has a recorded history dating back more than 3000 years, and it can make a valid case as the cradle of modern civilization. Its people are a blend of Mediterranean blood from North and South, East and West. Discovered and dated ruins go back thousands of years. Instead of calling the island's inhabitants Sicilian, might one suggest they be called "Mediterranean"? Benjamin suggests that "So many remains of ancient civilizations are scattered around Sicily that archaeologists call it 'Europe's museum'." Equally as telling, Mandela and Alio say that "... the Sicilians can lay a plausible claim to having the oldest society in Europe to be identified continuously from megalithic times until the modern era;" further adding that "The Sicilians are descended from the peoples of at least a dozen civilizations."

Sicily is the most often conquered piece of real estate on the planet! This fact alone speaks volumes about resilience, and is testimony to perseverance, adaptability and survival. If you had lived there at any time during the last two or three thousand years, these characteristics were a necessity.

Today, there is a great interest in genealogy, and the origin of one's roots. This interest has spawned an entire industry, as more and more people choose to have their DNA tested. DNA testing of a Sicilian, or an Italian from the foot of the boot, would probably reveal a complex mixture of blood lines of Galls, Normans and Romans from the North and West, Carthaginians, Tunisians and other Africans from the South, and Greeks, Turks and Byzantines from the East, plus a smattering of others who had access to the Mediterranean Sea. Because of its strategic location at the center of the Mediterranean region, and its navigable harbors, it became a desired and important intersection for trade, settlement, defense and eventually agriculture. To be able to categorize or define one as a true Sicilian, only the most modern of descriptions could be used.

Sicily undoubtedly has the most multi-cultural population of anywhere in the world, with perhaps the exception of the United States. Over thousands of years Sicily has evolved; but when two cultures collide, as it did so many times over in Sicily, it only took nine months, less than one year, to merge them. Thus, "Mediterraneans" evolved over hundreds of centuries, and to label them so may be the highest compliment we could pay them.

To help understand the meaning of multicultural-ism, here are two brief passages from the Mendola/Alio book:

> "The term multicultural describes the pres-ence of several distinct cultures in time, with so-cial equality guaranteed to persons of each culture. Sicily's language, traditions and even its cuisine have been shaped by its multicultural heritage. Call it a grand experiment, and call all who share its ideal 'Sicilian.'"

> "Culture, with its nuances and idiosyncra-sies, is what makes each of us different from each other. Were it not for our distinguishing cultures, we would all be the same. Culture is personality. It is humanizing. It touches every one of us. A cele-bration of cultural diversity is a celebration of our-selves, for to appreciate the culture of others is to enrich our own."

Most Americans have formed their opinions about Sicily, or gained their knowledge of it, because of the Mafia and the steady stream of films and television shows about the Cosa Nostra. The predominant contrib-utor is probably the movie "The Godfather" by Francis Ford Coppola. His Italian roots are in Basilicata, the re-gion (state) just north of Calabria. The Mafia is alive and well in southern Italy, and especially in Calabria where it is called "Ndrangheta." It is the most powerful Mafia in all of Italy, more powerful than the Sicilian Mafia, the

Neapolitan "Camorra" and the "Sacra Corona Unita" in Apulia. Its tentacles reach all of Europe, and into Africa, North and South America, and even to Australia and New Zealand. Its membership is estimated to be 6,000.

The Mafia has dominated the Sicilian criminal and political scene for hundreds of years, and its influence is actually the result of the island's multi-cultural character, with so many ethnic and religious forces at play simultaneously, and a patchwork legal system developed over time; but one that all could not agree upon or adapt to. Thus, an "underworld" government took hold to maintain some sort of order, although corrupt, illegal and ruthless.

And with the movement of more than five million Sicilians and other Italians to the United States, the Mafia came with them. If you grew up in an American Italian family during the 20th century, you obviously learned about the Mafia, and possibly even were somehow touched by it. But the Mafia is a much more modern institution in Sicily; and prior to the Mafia, Sicily developed with the benefit of influences from the greatest intellectual minds of the time, whether they be Greek, Roman, Byzantine, Jewish or Arab. Sicily was a place where learning from all these sources merged: a crossroads of the mind.

To suggest that Sicily was intellectually unsophisticated during its multicultural development over the last two thousand years is a gross misconception. The opposite is true. Byzantine culture there promoted civility, and the Byzantines went to great lengths to preserve much of Greek and Roman learning. Mendola/Alio conclude "Although we have no reliable figures, such evidence as can be garnered suggests that general literacy in Sicily under the Byzantine Greeks was higher than in most of Europe and that it increased further under the Arabs."

By around the year 900, Sicily was under the control of the Arabs, and Islam was its official religion. Christianity and Judaism were tolerated, but many of these non-believers converted to avoid harsh treatment. "...it must be said that Arab society and culture were advanced; under the Saracens, Palermo's splendor was said to rival that of Bagdad," say Mendola/Alio. But by the middle of the 11th century, Sicily's population was divided about equally between Christians and Muslims (90 percent), and the other 10 percent Jewish. One must remember that Jews were then defined by their genealogical roots in the Middle East.

According to Mendola/Alio "In the Middle Ages the ethnonym 'Jew' referred not simply to a religion, Judaism, but to those descended from Jews whose Semitic origin was rooted in the ancient society and culture of the Hebrews and Israelites. The religion and ethnic identity were the same."

One of the most interesting periods in Sicily's evolution occurred in the 11th and 12th centuries when in 1061 Robert de Hauteville, a Norman lord, accompanied by knights from Normandy, Lombardy and southern Italy captured the Arab garrison at Messina. Over the next 10 years the control of Sicily was secured by de Hauteville, and Sicily was once again a part of Europe. Robert's younger brother Roger, later in control, was labeled the "Count of Sicily" by his followers and "Emir of Emirs" by the Arabs.

"His rule also brought with it increased religious

freedom, greater artistic expression and a sovereign government," according to Mendola/Alio. He established a feudal system and governed with a tolerance, effectively creating "medieval Europe's greatest social experiment." The Normans even embraced certain Byzantine, Jewish and Muslim principles. The authors quoted above contend that Islamic law in Sicily was rather sophisticated; and they say there is evidence that portions were exported to England to "...form the basis of early common law."

In 1130, Roger II became king of Sicily and, from Palermo, ruled over all of Sicily, most of Italy south of Rome and parts of Tunisia. It was Europe's wealthiest realm, and there was peace among Christians, Muslims and Jews, as each group was permitted to be judged by its own laws. In their book, authors Mendola/Alio describe Roger II's kingdom with these words:

> "It would not be an exaggeration to describe the kingdom of Sicily Under the reign of Roger II as the most important realm of Europe and the Mediterranean, intellectually as well as politically. This halcyon era was a prosperous one. The royal revenues from Palermo alone exceeded those of all England."

Historian Giuseppe Greco describes this period of tranquility with these words: "The Normans gave to Southern Italy an atmosphere of serenity and of peace, after the scary nightmares unleashed by the Saracens. On the lands of Calabria rose a dawn of awakening, of enthusiasm, of activity."

But as we know, this was not to last, as intolerance again took foothold; and historians place the end of Sicily's multicultural experiment as the "turning point" year of 1282. The Crusades were in play; and by the middle of the 15th century, the Inquisition was in full swing, lasting some 300 years in Sicily. Many Jews fled Spain, Portugal and Sicily, making their way to remote parts of Southern Italy, thinking to be out of reach of the Roman Catholic Church and the Inquisition. But eventually, most of the Jews in southern Italy converted to Catholicism out of the need to persevere, adapt and survive.

The Character Of Southern Italians

It is difficult, at best, to genetically distinguish between the people from the southern most regions of the Italian peninsula (Calabria, Puglia and Basilicata) and Sicilians. However similar they may be genetically, there are defining differences in their traditions, folklore and cuisine. The migrations, back and forth, over the centuries was commonplace; and although most today are Roman Catholic, that was not always the case. Jewish and Islamic practices have woven their way into the Catholicism of today's southern Italy.

I took a day to venture across the Strait of Messina for a visit to that Sicilian city as an effort to see what differences I might find. My investigation was short and based only on my own observations and random discussions with people in cafes and on the street. The results of this brief excursion are discussed later in Chapter VII. In many ways, Calabria is a mirror reflection of Sicily; it shares many of the same conquests and foreign interventions. As we examine the characteristics of

Calabrians, and southern Italians, you will note that their lives were often much harsher due to the poorer agricultural practices and the less organized and absentee governance; and with these conditions over long periods of time their perseverance and resilience became acute. Others would disagree, saying the two are not reflective of each other. Michael Caputo, in his book "The Coin From Calabria" says that at no time in history did any foreign "country" or party control all of Calabria. True, Calabria was invaded by outsiders, but this control was scattered; and Calabrians, in their constant struggle for survival, simply moved around, mostly inland from the coasts. In his book, he wrote of the Saracen incursions from Sicily: "Calabrians response to the Saracen arrival was to simply move inland, which is the main reason why countless villages were created on the mountainous regions, away from the coast." Caputo concludes, "In spite of relentless incursions, Calabria stood firm against the brutal Saracens. The Orthodox Byzantines, the Catholic Normans and the fiery Calabrians, created a barrier the Saracens tried to totally penetrate in vain. Finally, they were pushed back into their ships and were "forced to go back to where they originated from."

The Calabrian village that Caputo's family came from is only about 20 miles west of Serrastretta, with a very similar landscape. Its history suggests that it was first settled by a group of Basilian, Greek speaking monks that left areas of Sicily and the Byzantine Empire to escape Muslin rule. Other Basilian monks came to parts of central Calabrian and established many monasteries. Caputo suggests that over hundreds of years, Calabria was more devastated by earthquakes than by foreign domination. Caputo tells of the period, under Napoleon rule when his family's village was scheduled to be destroyed, which it was, and "...my people were forced to rebuild the town, once again, just as they had twenty-three years earlier as a result of the 1783 earthquakes. And this they did with much patience and resilience."

Caputo concludes his book with the following words:

> "These are my people – and they are me. I share their weaknesses but I also share their strengths. And now, more than ever, I am very glad to be the descendant of the strong, courageous and resilient people of that special and beautiful land, Calabria."

Calabria today is home to just under two million people and is comprised of 5,800 square miles. It is bordered on the north by Basilicata, on the east by the Ionian Sea, on the west by the Tyrrhenian Sea, and on the south by the Mediterranean. Many small resort villages dot both coasts, while running down the center of the "foot" is a long mountain range which is often blanketed with snow in the winter. The highest peaks average between three and five thousand feet. Sicily is in clear view of Calabria, especially from the higher elevations, and the island's Messina is only a few miles across the water channel. Like Sicily, Calabria is literally a museum and filled with the ruins of its long-ago inhabitants.

That describes the land mass of Calabria, but our interest is in its people. Most of the Calabrian people have Sicilian roots, and their genealogy, therefore, is multicultural and predominantly Greek.

In the Prologue to his book "Calabrian Tales," author

Peter Chiarella used some very well-chosen words to describe Calabrians. In talking about the Roman conquest of the region in the third century BC which "...began a protracted period of domination by a series of conquerors," Chiarella states that "Calabrians aspirations were dashed so often by intruders that a fatalistic character was embedded in their psyche over the centuries."

The author goes on to say, "Not only was the Calabrian sentenced to a thankless life of drudgery, but his work was performed under dangerous and adverse conditions." He states that "Growth and progress were measured by how well the family survived." Chiarella's book covers the period 1860 to 1920, the period when many Calabrians came to America. He concludes in his Prologue, "Their progeny has made it a part of the landscape of America. This period was a period in Italian history following the unification of the many foreign-dominated Italian states into the kingdom of Italy. It was a time of great pride in a new nation, coupled with intense poverty and struggle."

Chiarella weaves some interesting tales whose characters seem to be masters of perseverance, adaptability and survival. It is almost as if they were blessed with minimal expectations to match the results they achieved. These people had much in common beyond their meager existence. They valued the land before it became scarce; they understood organic before it became fashionable; they prized their children without giving them trophies; and they had faith in a higher power without questioning authority. And for Italy and its people, regardless of northern or southern, the sea was and is as much of a pathway to the future as the land. They are forever entwined.

In her book *CALABRIA, The Other Italy,* author Karen Haid observed "Italians the entire length of the peninsula lament over the lack of opportunities for young people, low wages and the excessive joblessness. In Calabria, these problems are exacerbated to the point of being an ordinary component of daily life. Nevertheless, they resent being viewed as a burden by northerners and often point to unification as a negative turning point for their economy...Of course, everything wasn't rosy for the average peasant before unification, either, but Calabrians feel that they have been too severely judged on an unfair playing field."

Since 1856, Italy is a unified country comprised of 18 regions including the entire peninsula, Sicily and Sardinia; but to Italians, this is a recent development. Over the centuries, Italy has been under a great many dominating influences, both foreign and domestic, and today it is controlled by three powerful entities: the Italian government, the Vatican, and the Mafia. Effectively, they co-govern, while the majority of Italians have a distaste for and a mistrust of all three. Given Italy's history, this is understandable. Tolerating all three is a way of life for Italians, and as long as they have their freedom, their resilience will take care of the rest.

As I put the finishing touches on this first chapter, I am in the air on the way to Rome, and on the way to Lamezia Terme in Calabria. I plan to spend the first month or two learning the landscape, investigating and getting to know the municipality of Serrastretta and its surrounding villages. What I find will be discussed in a later chapter, but my research will uncover, not only the physical environment that exists there, but the character of the people who inhabit these small villages, averaging 200 to 500 residents each. I will be searching for the surviving descendents of the five Serrastretta founding families, one of which (Scalise) is my own.

CHAPTER II:

The Author's First Days In Calabria

(I Primi Giorne Dell'Autore In Calabria)

"I would rather know than to be."
— Leonardo da Vinci

In the newest autobiography of Leonardo da Vinci, author Norman Isaacson observed: "Being relentlessly and randomly curious about everything around us is something that each of us can push ourselves to do, every waking hour, just as he did." As Isaacson suggests, I am constantly observing and questioning.

In writing this chapter, I was confident this material will help the reader better understand "resilience," since I keep a detailed daily journal; and I now travel to Italy (possibly to stay), as my grandfather Rosario Bevevino travelled to America in 1902 (to stay). He often said he would never go back because "I have nothing to go back for." This the reader will come to understand as the story unfolds. I am making his journey in reverse and returning home for him; he to America in 1902, I to Calabria in 2018, 116 years later. So, I am proud to be here, as he was proud to go to America.

And now it begins. I arrived at the airport in Lamezia Terme on Tuesday, May 22, 2018 and awaited my host Sonia Bellezza (P1). She arrived an hour late and we then drove to her home 15 minutes away. My first impressions were not unexpected since I had seen photos of her home and its surroundings in advance. Sonia and I got along wonderfully as we had come to know each other well through the exchange of hundreds of emails over the six months before my arrival. Once there, I was dead tired after my 24-hour journey, door to door, without sleep. Very quickly after only one day there, Sonia and I concluded her home was not the best place for me because it is too remote from the town center of Lamezia Terme and a 45-minute drive to Serrastretta. We agreed that I needed to locate myself in Serrastretta, and she has friends there who will immediately begin looking for an accommodation.

I stayed at her home for three nights until she found a room for me at an *"agritourismo"* very close to Serrastretta. It has three very well-appointed rooms, virtually new, and there are more being built. It is owned and operated by a large family that lives in several adjacent houses. The owner/manager Marco Molinaro is a professional chef, and on weekends, he serves many large family luncheons and dinners in two beautiful dining rooms. This was my new residence for three days, so I was forced to enjoy it; but I ate and drank well, went for walks and caught up on my sleep. The only whiskey the bar stocked was scotch, so it replaced my usual vodka. The total cost of the three days, including room, meals and cocktails, was 150 Euro or about $180 – a good value but well above my estimated daily budget.

Sonia kept telling me in our phone conversations that someone would come to pick me up in the afternoon of the third day to take me to my next temporary housing, so I sat and waited from about 2:00pm on. Finally, a car pulled up with two men in it. The driver got out of the car and he was dressed as a priest in a full length medium blue robe with a red sash and red skull cap; I thought possibly Greek Orthodox. He came right up to me and said my name, so we loaded the car and off we went, but to where I had no idea.

We drove through dense, dark forests on some paved roads and others dirt, some so narrow two cars could not pass; and the thought flashed into my mind that I was being kidnapped into some mysterious Bavarian wood and we would end up at Dracula's castle. But no, after about 40 minutes we pulled into a group of buildings, under construction, and it was a new Catholic monastery, of what order I did not know. We went inside and were met by a nun in a similar habit to the priest's, and they escorted me to my room on the second floor, saying dinner would be at 8:00pm and they would come for me. I was at the Monastero San Benedetto Giuseppe Labre (P2) near the town of Decollatura.

I felt totally confused, but safe, thinking how would I ever get out of here if I had to; the monastery is too remote to walk anywhere, and which direction would I take? I thought: well, here I am, and I must make the best of it. In hindsight, I felt like a true Calabrian, facing adversity and called upon to use my resilience, perseverance and adaptability to get by.

I was privileged to have dinner with members of the order at their table in the large kitchen. Present were the priest who picked me up, Don Benedetto, and three nuns, along with a volunteer couple who worked there. One of the three nuns was the mother/abbot of the monastery, also with the name Benedetta; and the other two nuns were Sister Latizia and Sister Aurora. Sister Latizia spoke rather good English, and we had very open and cordial conversation. It was an honor to be with them, they telling me I was a special guest and family. All of them know Sonia Bellezza, and I have the sense that she stayed with them for some type of rehabilitation. During our dinner conversation I learned the monastery's mission is to care for people with mental issues or marital problems, those needing a retreat and rehabilitation. They also house about 22 African migrants from six different countries who are waiting there to have their Italian entry status resolved.

The following morning I was up very early, had to take a cold shower, and then got dressed and went for a walk. Breakfast was at 7:00am, and again we had very cordial conversation. They loved to discuss politics which I did not engage in. At 10:00am they came for me, as we were now leaving to see Don Luigi Iuliano, pastor of the Catholic Church in Serrastretta. I later learned he is pastor emeritus, and the pastor of another church in Lamezia Terme, about 45 minutes away. We arrived at Don Luigi's home (P3,4) in about 20 minutes, and he greeted us in the driveway. He escorted us inside and served us iced tea (cold, but without ice) and the conversation began. Sister Latizia sat next to me and translated. Later I learned Don Luigi is simply known to everyone as Don Gigi.

Sister Latezia translated about 20 minutes of casual conversation; then the two priests and the nun go off for a private conversation. We were shown the house and I was asked to pick the bedroom I wanted. I chose the one at the end of a wing extending out from the very back of the house. It has its own patio area and overlooks a field and orchard in back; and it has a bathroom, but no shower, so I must use one of the bathrooms inside the main house to shower. To completely describe the home would take far too many pages; in short it is very large, very well appointed, and is filled with many religious artifacts, paintings, tapestries and antiquities. It must be at least 8,000 square feet, has seven bedrooms, five bath rooms and an elongated dining table that seats 22(P5), and its own chapel. The other spaces I will not even begin to describe. It is Don Gigi's family home, and it was first constructed in 1667, although little of the original structure remains.

Don Gigi and Don Benedetto do not speak English, so Sister Latizia translates for me. After more light, cordial discussion, the three of them go off for another private talk, returning after 30 minutes. Sister Latizia tells me the deal is done and I can stay here. I asked her how much I should pay, and she then questioned me "How much do you want to pay?" Having to think quickly on my feet, I told her my pre-arrival budget was 15 Euro per day. She informs Don Gigi, comes back and tells me "The deal is done including all meals." I guess I hit a home run.

Upon leaving, Don Bededetto and Sister Latizia said

not to worry; that everything would be taken care of, including my need for an extended stay visa. They would help me in whatever way they could, and all I needed do is call upon them. I then said jokingly to the good sister that if I married here there would be no visa issue. She laughed, saying that was too extreme and could be bad for me. "There is good and bad in every marriage," I replied.

I was now in my fourth accommodation having arrived only six days earlier. It was just Don Gigi and me in this huge home, and I immediately thought how fortunate I was because this environment will provide a new learning experience and force me to improve my Italian language skill. The first thing he told me is that now we would eat lunch. He prepared a delicious meal of swordfish and other courses; and I watched him eat large portions very rapidly. We cleaned the table and went outside to enjoy a cigarette together. He then departed, telling me he would return at 8:00pm. This gave me the opportunity to explore the house and take a long, much needed nap, thinking to myself there are definite advantages being a priest in a small town in Italy.

The next days were filled with discovery as I learned to get along with Don Gigi and communicate with him. I was always observing and making mental and written notes. Several times a day I would make entries in my detailed daily journal. And I was able to go into the town center of Serrastretta and Angoli, the birthplace of my grandparents. On those outings, Don Gigi would drop me off, returning to pick me up three to five hours later. I was able to make new friends and meet relatives I previously did not know existed. Every day was filled with new discoveries. I learned very quickly that I must constantly monitor my next foot step because level ground is at a premium. This is not only true because of the steep mountain terrain, but more so due to the lack of construction and architectural standards when updating extremely old structures, particularly so when entering or exiting a building or stepping off a curb. There is no consistency (height or width) of steps; and when you go to use a bathroom (*"bagno"*), it is a challenge to find the light switch, not to speak of the paper products. Each facility is different, and the electrical wiring and switches are so diverse, you must leave the door open for enough light; and be sure to take off your sunglasses.

One of the first people I met in Serrastretta was Antonio Molinaro, with the same last name as the mayor and a local business man and financial consultant. Good fortune is at my side. He spoke some English and he came to understand my purpose here and my family connection. He offered to help me any way he could, and he would like to have lunch together one day soon at his favorite restaurant. I walked around town, checked out the market and then parked myself on a bench facing the church *(Maria Santissima Del Perpetuo Soccorso – Blessed Virgin Mary of Perpetual Help)*.

I was awaiting the arrival of Rabbi Barbara Aiello (a contact I had made three years ago), the first female Jewish rabbi in Italy, with a synagogue in Serrastretta. Ironically, she was born in Pittsburgh, Pennsylvania; and her parents and grandparents were born in Serrastretta, but moved to the United States in 1920. There will be much more about Rabbi Barbara in a subsequent chapter.

She telephoned me and said she would be with me

in a few minutes. We had a very fruitful conversation and agreed to meet at least twice for interview sessions to be featured in Chapter IV: "The Popular Priest, The Remarkable Rabbi And The Marvelous Mayor." In the little time I had been with her, it was easy to discern that she is more American than Italian, even though she holds dual citizenship and has been in Calabria for 21 years, the last 15 of those years full-time.

On the following day, I made my second visit to the village of Angoli to see Sabrina Mazzei Iuliano, a local school teacher who is fluent in English. Her maiden name is Mazzei. I was invited into her home (P6) which sits on the piazza, adjacent to and facing the church, San Giuseppi. She quickly came to understand my family history in Serrastretta and Angoli; and she also understood the purpose of my being here. She liked the idea of the book and offered her assistance any way she could. Most interesting is the fact that we are probably related for reasons that become clear in a later chapter.

During our conversation, I read her a passage from my daily journal, and I am repeating it here, quoting myself as follows:

> "Many of the homes in Angoli have a family photo outside the front door on the exterior wall. These photos are concrete evidence of the importance placed on family and the pride these people have in their ancestors, and the hundreds of years of Angoli history they created: another testimony to their resilience, their ability to persevere, adapt and survive. If an average American would visit here, he would think that time has passes these

people by. I suggest, however, that just the opposite is true. The comfort they have in knowing who they are and from where they came leads them to a peaceful existence without anxiety. Yet, they too can master modern technology, the computer and data communication; and they live in what is considered the poorest and most backward part of Italy in a tiny village seemingly from the past and in the middle of nowhere."

One might think that the children of Serrastretta and its villages are somehow disadvantaged, but just the opposite is true. Actually, they grow up in the best of all worlds with a good family, a safe environment, an adequate education from which many go on to a university, and a natural surrounding where the smallest things are treasured and appreciated.

When we concluded our conversation, she wanted to show me a "B&B" that she and her husband Massimo own. I agreed and thought we would be driving somewhere out of town. Instead, we walked across the piazza and down the street on the other side of the church stopping at a handsome door which Sabrina unlocked. We entered a newly constructed and appointed two floor apartment which she and Massimo rent to tourists for 15 Euro per day. She showed me around; the entry room is small, has a drop-down table stored in the wall and a hidden kitchen behind bifold doors complete with gas range, microwave, counter and refrigerator. Behind this entry room is a large bathroom with shower, toilet, bidet and clothes washing machine. Upstairs is the bedroom with a large bed and closet space.

Sabrina said I could stay at the apartment if I wanted. "Yes," I said. "It would be perfect for me." We came to a tentative agreement that I would rent it starting in September. The only disadvantages I could see is it not being in Serrastretta proper, and the stairs are very steep with the bathroom downstairs. These are not too big to overcome, and the good part is I could cook for myself which I enjoy doing.

When I am in Serrastretta, I usually hang out at the Fazio Wine Bar or the Gallo Pasticceria & Café/Bar to meet new friends, always observing and learning. *"Pasticceria"* is a pastry shop, and their Italian croissants are to die for. It is now day 12 since my arrival, and while sitting outside in front of Gallo's, I again ran into my friend Antonio Molinaro. He had his beautiful eight-year-old daughter with him. We chatted briefly and he again offered his assistance, especially with seeing the mayor, but with anything else I needed. He should prove to be a great contact and resource.

The next day was Sunday, and I had the full intention of going to mass, hopefully in Serrastretta. But no, I was to accompany Don Gigi to his parish in Lamezia, but little did I know I would I be there all day. I dressed in jacket and tie for the first time in months. We arrived at 7:30am at Chiesa Del Carmine, and he told me to meet him back at the car parked behind the church at 12:30pm. I thought we would then return home for a nice Sunday meal. The day, however, turned out totally different.

Don Gigi said mass at 8:00am, which I attended. His sermon was powerful, which I could discern because of his voice inflection and his hand and arm gestures; although I could not understand a word of it. He said a second mass at 10:00am, and I went across the street to the coffee bar to hang out and meet new friends. Little did I know that Don Gigi would perform a wedding mass at 11:00am. While at the coffee bar I struck up conversations with the four others sitting there, only one of which spoke very little English. Men would come in and out for a coffee, but at no time was it crowded, not yet anyway. Speaking of men and church, each of the two masses were attended by about 100 parish members, only 10 to 15 percent men, typical of Italy.

While sitting outside at the coffee bar, a car pulls up and the man next to me says the driver speaks very good English. He comes over and I am introduced to Luigi (Louie) Trombetta. His English was perfect, and he explained to me that he and his parents moved to Chicago when he was 15, now having returned after 30 years there. He owns a small deli just a few doors down the street from the church. We engage in great conversation, as it is now approaching 11:00am, and I noticed suddenly the terrace in front of the coffee bar is flooded with men; so much so that I cannot see past them and view the front of the church. They are there to see all the beautiful young women arriving for the wedding, and, of course, to watch the bride enter the church. The bride does not arrive until 11:40am (typical of Calabrian time), and she pulls up in a beautiful silver Alfa Romeo top down sports car.

The wedding commences, and the 12:30pm hour arrives, so I walk around to the back of the church to find that Don Gigi's car is not there; I return to the front of the church, enter, and find that Don Gigi was not at the alter, but rather another priest. But where did he go? Did he leave me behind and return home for his important lunch? I have observed how much he enjoys eating. At no time did I panic, but instead, called on my resilience. Well, if this be the case, my only option is to take an expensive cab ride back to Serrastretta. As I am standing there considering my one option, he pulls up in his car and motions me to get in. I felt rescued.

We drove a few blocks away and he parks on the street. Of course, you must understand that he speaks to me very little because he gets frustrated when I cannot understand, and it shows. We went to an apartment building and he rang to be let in. We are greeted at the door of an apartment on the second floor, and I realize we are there for the mid-day Sunday meal. After enjoying a six-course delicious "lunch," we return to the church; and to my surprise discover that Don Gigi will conduct a 4:00pm funeral mass. I waited outside until it concludes, and then I am driven home by the two men we had lunch with. Don Gigi never returned until 10:00pm. What a long day for the both of us, especially him.

Monday is Don Gigi's day of rest, taking naps but still busying himself with house chores. He did take the time to leave for a dentist appointment. I informed him that I was almost out of cigarettes and we must go to town for more. He also smokes, but he emphatically told me "no," saying I smoke too much and drink too much vodka; and I will be doing penance. He did share one with me and we sat outside each enjoying a smoke before retiring.

The following morning, we drive to town at 9:00am, he drops me off and instruct me to go buy my vodka and cigarettes, and a pack for him. We immediately returned home. Without the benefit of any real conversation with him, I will describe him in some detail. Just this morning after I said *"buon giurno"* to him, I jokingly suggested that he had too much *"vino"* last evening at some reunion party he went to because he slept in so long. He quickly retorted that I had too much vodka and gives me the sign of the cross. Then he tells me by gesture, placing his hand over his head and wiggling his fingers like water falling that it is time for me to shower.

Don Gigi is a very kind and generous man, with a good sense of humor, but his character is far different with me than with others, particularly his parishoners. He uses a much softer tone of voice with them, and with me, he speaks loudly, caused by his frustration that I do not understand what he is saying in Italian. It is as if he was speaking to a person who is hard of hearing, wearing an aid. Out of his frustration he has nicknamed me *"stupido,"* but I simply laugh when he uses it. To describe him further I will elaborate on some words I used earlier. The best words to use are "compulsive" and "obsessive." He is constantly busy, repeating tasks and chores that need no repeating, whether that be sweeping, moping, hosing down, whatever. Anal he is, and I have come to understand why. Living in this large house alone, he is in fear of an idle mind and body, and where that that may lead him. I understand this through my own experiences; and I believe very few others have gotten as close to him as I have these last two weeks. I have observed that he spends no time during the day in prayer or meditation, like cloistered monks do in a monastery.

It is now my 17th day in Calabria, and this morning

Don Gigi became very frustrated, seeming to object to my wanting to go into the town center of Serrastretta, or him having to drive me there. I said I would walk the four or five kilometers even though it takes two hours. At least it is all down-hill, but I could not make the walk back. He begrudgingly said he would take me immediately. No words were spoken on the 10-minute drive. He dropped me off at least 500 yards short of town center. I said "grazie" as I got out of the car, but he never smiled or said a word.

I was in town from 10:30am until 5:30pm and had a very productive day in addition to eating a light lunch. I ran into my friend Antonio Molinaro who agreed to help me secure a cheap car which I desperately need. Next, I walked to the City Hall, introduced myself to the receptionist and asked to see the mayor, Felice Molinaro. I was taken to the second floor, and a gentleman there who spoke some English, phoned the mayor. I was told he would return in 10 minutes to see me. We then went to the third floor and was asked to wait in the reception area just outside his office. Seated, I began to wonder if the mayor's 10 minutes would turn out to be 30 or 45 minutes.

He arrived on schedule, and we ended up having a very fruitful half-hour conversation. He spoke much better English than I expected since I had emailed him several times before arriving in Calabria and he never responded. He told me he was excited about my book project, and I would have his full support and cooperation. We made a formal appointment for next week when I will be accompanied by Sabrina to translate. The absolute best thing he said to me was he loved the title and concept of this book, and that the people of Serrastretta epitomize resilience and the character it takes to persevere, adapt and survive. He is obviously very proud of his town and its people.

I walked out of his office feeling I had scored a major victory, and went to find some lunch, a *"panino"* with Calabrian salami and cheese; and I await the next meeting with the mayor having high expectations.

I will fast forward a bit, and it is now my 39th day in Calabria. One week earlier, I moved into the newly renovated B&B of Sabrina Mazzei Iuliano, a cousin, in Angoli, and it suits my needs perfectly as it is in the center of town and has a complete kitchen and the local restaurant/bar is just 10 doors away providing a perfect place to meet new people and discover new things about my surroundings. I look forward to each new day and the challenges to be faced and overcome.

On my 43rd day in Calabria, I took the opportunity to travel to northern Italy and visit friends who live near Milan. I spent two days with Giuseppe and Lucia Morell, a wonderful couple I have known for 25 years. We spent a great amount of time catching up on our families, talking about our genealogies and discussing work on this book. Giuseppe has researched his Italian family back to the time of Charlemagne and he is extremely proud of his ancestry, some having the blood of royalty. The Morells used the term *"questitone meridronale,"* a reference to the people of southern Italy needing help and support, then receiving it from the government and the mafia. More political votes, they said, come from the south than from the north, and most post office and teaching jobs in the north go to people from the south;

yet there is great respect for the hard-working people from the south. My friends view southern Italians as very clever, saying they figure out how to earn a living for their family because this mentality is instilled in them; while in the north, families think about teaching their children to find good employment to provide for themselves.

One of the academics I spoke with during my research in Italy observed "People in the north of Italy are quick to suggest the Italian economy is weak and lagging, but Calabrians and others in the south do not complain about it, because to them, it has never been this good."

Prior to my travel here, I did a great amount of reading and internet research about Calabria and Serrastretta. There was nothing, no text, no pictures, no videos that could have prepared me for what I discovered here in person. From the mountainous landscape, to the deep lush forests, to the architecture, to the centuries old crumbling structures, everything was a revelation. What I was not surprised by are the people, their warmth, their friendliness, and their unwavering attitude of taking life as it comes. It is now time to conclude this chapter as I think about my first days of discovery that will always continue, through constant observation, hopefully until my last breath. My extensive study of Leonardo da Vinci has been of great assistance to me; and this realization is now more meaningful than ever as I complete this work in 2019, the 500th anniversary of his passing.

CHAPTER III:

Serrastretta And Its Surrounding Villages

(Serrastretta E I Suoi Villaggi Circostanti)

"What a better teacher than history,
To be its witness, live its mysteries.
Reaching back to a better time and place,
To study life at a much slower pace.
The magic in all its simplicity,
Greatness I can then even touch and see.
I might tire of this chosen road
But treasure the learning I did unfold."

The Author
— From "Reaching For The Light"

Serrastretta, with a population of about 3,500, sits squarely in the center of the foot of Italy's boot, just below the ankle. It is in the middle of the mountain range that runs north-south through the center of Italy. The mountains are heavily forested and lush green, and their altitude is between 3,000 and 5,000 feet above sea level. Serrastretta is at 3,000 feet, and on a clear day you can see Sicily to the southwest, the Tyrrhenian and Mediterranean Seas to the west and the Ionian Sea to the east. Serrastretta's highest population count was about 17,000 some 100 or more years ago.

To reach Serrastretta from the coast, you must climb steeply on narrow winding roads that have switchbacks at least every 200 to 300 yards; and the views to the valley below on the way up are spectacular. In many places the road is covered by a canopy of trees, so dense in places that no sunlight comes through, as if you were driving through a tunnel with no illumination. It reminds me of driving the Pennsylvania Turnpike 60 years ago. The city of Lamezia Terme on the plain below, (P7), with a population of 70,000, is very near the western coast. The drive from there, where the airport is situated, takes about 45 minutes covering a distance of about 20 miles (32 kilometers). The residents of the mountain villages must go to Lamezia Terme for major shopping or work, mostly working service jobs at the many shops and resort hotels along the sea. Once you have reached the higher elevations and the mountain villages, you have placed yourself in a pristine environment (P8) where there is no roadside litter, no writings on roadside buildings or walls, unlike lower down the mountain; and you are saddened when a few trees along the road must be removed to prevent them from falling.

Once you get to Serrastretta, you enter a completely different world where the pace of life is slow, the surroundings are very tranquil, the people are warm and friendly; and everything by USA standards is "artisan," and virtually everything grown locally is "organic." This includes from the way the farming is done to the making of bread, cheese, salami, furniture and pizza. The people here discovered organic before organic was discovered. It is not unusual to come across a shepherd and his dog crossing the road with his small herd of goats or sheep (P9); and you may even see pack mules being used. You literally have the sensation of stepping back in time. There are no taxis in Serrastretta, but there is a bus back and forth to Lamezia Terme a few times a day. With little traffic, people stroll down the middle of the main street. It is a quiet, peaceful and tranquil place. The local roads and streets are two-lane with no berms, no designated parking spaces or stop signs (none that are adhered to), and one-way traffic is on demand. On Sundays the two coffee bars are packed, and the people coming into the coffee bars or walking the street look rather prosperous and are well-dressed. Serrastretta is also very busy on Fridays when 10 to 15 venders line the main street at the north end selling everything from fruits, vegetables, men's and women's clothing, shoes, linens, handbags, etc.

Serrastretta is best known commercially for its woodworking (P10), and particularly the manufacture of cane seat chairs; it is known as "The City of the Chair" *(Citta Della Sedia)*. Men cut and assemble the pieces for the solid wood chairs while women sit and literally weave the reed seats onto the assembled chair. The reeds are grown in local marsh areas; and I can recall as a child watching my grandfather weave baskets of all sizes from reeds he cultivated in marshy areas along the railroad tracks in northwestern Pennsylvania. He obviously learned the skill as a young boy growing up in Serrastretta. To this day, I treasure the few of his basket I have.

In the town center of Serrastrett a(P11), dominated by

the church of the *Beata Maria Vergine del Soccorso* (dating back to 1395) and its piazza, there is a sizable chain grocery store, two other smaller markets (with deli), a meat market, a tobacco shop, two coffee bars (one a *"pasticceria"* or pastry shop), a bank, a pharmacy, a farm supply/nursery store, barber shop, beauty shops, cosmetics shop, jewelry store and two gas stations (with deli). And, of course, City Hall, a post office and a police station. There is a total of five policemen *(carrabinieri)* responsible for Serrastretta and its surrounding villages, and a couple of Serrastretta in-town policemen. Here, you never see anyone argue or be rude to another; and you do not have to guard your wallet. The entire town is a beautiful place, picturesque and pristine, with its tree lined main street of brick pavers, the large church, handsome city hall and well kept, refurbished homes. People regularly walk down the middle of the main street, even with their baby strollers. Of course, there are old structures appearing to date from hundreds of years ago. Everything appears well maintained and clean. The town is also birthplace of one of Italy's most famous and popular contemporary singers. She is Dalida, who was at the peak of her career between 1960 and 1980. Her name is Iolanda Cristina Gigliotti, and ironically enough, in 1883 a woman by the name of Maria Gigliotti of Serrastretta was the midwife at my grandfather's birth. Maria also signed and was witness to the civil registration of birth filed here at the City Hall the day following his birth on June 5, 1883 in the nearby village of Angoli.

The name of Serrastretta's church alone speaks volumes; the church of the Blessed Virgin Mary of Perpetual Help.

Police in Italy are varied and have different respon-sibilities and authority. For example, *carrabinieri* are national police and a part of the Italian military, while another national police force with major facilities in the larger cities *(Commissariato Di Polizia Di Lamezia Terme)* have authority over immigration; and the smaller towns and villages have their own small force employed by the municipality, but they have limited jurisdiction. *Carabinieri* and *Commissariato Di Polizia* facilities are very secure, fenced-in locations with highly sophisticat-ed communications capability.

There are many residents here with the same last name (Scalise, Gallo, Fazio, Mazzei, Molinaro, to name just a few), but not many claim to be relatives. The rea-son for this has a simple explanation; beginning with the first five families here 800 years ago; they inter-mar-ried and more new families arrived. Over time, the fam-ilies with the same last name became diluted, so if you were many generations removed, you would not be considered related. Think of it as a centuries old huge tree with a very large trunk at its base (Scalise/Fazio, for example), and you were a branch on this tree hundreds of feet in the air. You would not be related to a similar branch on the other side of the tree even though your last name is the same.

The Catholic Church in Serrastretta has a huge dou-ble central door, 12 to 15 feet tall (P12,13), and on those double doors are 12 sculpted metal panels depicting life in Serrastretta. On the left-hand main door there is a man plowing with oxen, two priests greeting, a man, his wife and child tending a pig, two women harvesting olives, a woman catching chestnuts falling from a tree, and a man and woman dancing. On the right-hand main door, a woman holding her child next to suitcases while her husband is embracing someone in the background, a woman weaving a chair seat with reeds, two carpenters cutting wood, a woman weaving fabric on a loom, and two blacksmiths at work. On the two smaller doors that flank the main doors, there are more raised sculptures. On the left door there is an embryo in a womb and a pair of hands raising up a baby. On the right door is a bouquet of wheat and grape leaves and a dove carrying an olive branch. You marvel at these 16 pieces of sculpted art, and you have not even walked inside yet. What more than these church doors could give testimony to Calabrians strong belief in procreation and family, religion and faith, and nature itself. With this alone, my case could be rested.

Serrastretta does have a Jewish synagogue, several museums and a well-preserved castle ruins dating back to the 16th century when the Spanish ruled here. Speaking of dates, between the years 1283 and 1300, the town originated and was first settled by five Jewish families coming out of Sicily to escape the Inquisition of the Catholic Church when Sicily was under Spain's control. As mentioned earlier in a previous chapter, the five families were Bruni, Fazio, Mancuso, Scalise and Talarico. I am a direct Scalise descendant; and virtually all the descendants of these families, after the first 100 years, converted to Catholicism out of the need to survive as the Roman church spread south from Naples. Yet some Jews remain today forced over the years to hide their ancestral religion in the "closet," or more precisely in the basement. Over many years there was a blending of Jewish and Catholic traditions, some of which survive today in Calabria.

Just think about it for a moment. Serrastretta was here, as an active community, 200 years before the Renaissance took full root in northern Italy, and 200 years before Columbus first sailed to America. The rulers of Spain and the Roman Catholic Church were the driving force behind the persecution and migration of Jews in Sicily and southern Italy, while at the same time sponsoring Columbus (an Italian) and his expeditions. It caused the Jews to spread to all parts of Italy, looking for a place where they would be welcome; instead they often found more persecution and ghettos. And today, we see Jewish populations dwindle in both Europe and North America; and attempts in the USA to dishonor Columbus for his maltreatment of native Americans; yet up to 40 percent of all Calabrians have Jewish roots. An irony for certain created by man against man in the name of some higher power. Through all of this, what occurred over the last 700 years, Sicilians and Calabrians have had to call upon their resilience to persevere, adapt and ultimately survive. These characteristics are to be honored and revered; and every one of their descendants living today should pray they inherited a trace of it. Speaking for myself, I am proud to be of Calabrian descent and a Roman Catholic of Jewish roots as the first Christians were.

In its early history, the town of Serrastretta grew in population between 1300 and 1500, and the farmable land around it could no longer support its residents; and hence the surrounding villages were created. Groups of families ventured out. Observing Serrastretta today, you immediately notice the shortage of level land, crops having to be planted on terraced steps up and down the hillsides. The Scalise family, for example, was one in a group that established Angoli, about three miles away to the southeast. It is up the mountain from Serrastretta, and down the other side. Built into a steep hillside, probably chosen because of its supply of water. Its creation is another example of perseverance, adaptability and survival. Just to carve out the road on those hillsides with multiple switchback turns was a major feat itself. I have driven the few miles between Serrastretta and Angoli and it takes longer than expected. My grandfather took a similar ride the day he was born in 1883, and it took the party including Maria Gigliotti, Brigida Scalise, infant Rosario and probably a horse drawn cart driver hours to make the journey from Angoli to Serrastretta, as the written city hall record testifies to their 9:11pm arrival. It was, however, explained to me that you could make the journey in two hours on foot by using the trails through the forest as many of the early residents did to reach their distant gardens. The building housing the foundling home in Serrastretta where Rosario was placed on the "wheel" is still there today, but the wheel is gone.

The current mayor of Serrastretta is Felice Molinaro, and he has pledged to me his full cooperation and support for this book. He loves the concept and the title; and he sat with me in his office for an interview. He loves the town and its people, and firmly believes they are unique in all of Calabria. A man of about 42 years of age, he oversees Serrastretta and all its surrounding villages from his office in the municipality headquarters building just down the main street from the church piazza.

There are 10 surrounding villages in all, each with a
population of between 80 to 400 residents, and each incorporated into the municipality of Serrastretta. The five
primary villages are Accario, Angoli, Cancello, Migliuso
and San Michele, all south and spread out east and west
of Serrastretta. To walk the 43 kilometer loop would take
more than 10 hours. Throughout the course of my research I visited each village. As I write this, I am making
plans to take up temporary residence in Angoli, further
embedding myself in the fabric of my resources, but I
will be cautiously driving back and forth between Angoli
and Serrastretta on a regular basis. The 13-kilometer-long
(eight mile) road between Serrastretta and Angoli has
so many curves that when driving it you are constantly
turning the steering wheel, and there are many places
along the way your car is headed in the exact opposite
direction you were driving just two seconds earlier. It
is hard to imagine driving these roads without power
steering. As you travel these serpentine roads between
the villages, it is not unusual to see a small flock of goats
or sheep crossing, tended by a farmer and his dog; or
you may witness the use of pack mules.

The town of Serrastretta and some of its villages are
adorned with a small fenced-in and landscaped park
area, each with three large white crosses. Christian religious symbols abound here. Everywhere you look,
you see reminders of how deeply rooted in the culture
Catholicism and faith are. The countryside is heavily
populated with religious shrines (P14), and you will find
them along the roadways, on buildings and houses,
stone walls and in grottos. I have even seen them af-
fixed to roadside guard rails and inside utility control

boxes on houses. In Calabria, there must be thousands; in Angoli alone, I counted more than 20.

The Village of Angoli

Once I took up residence in Angoli, it took no time at all to become part of village's fabric, as if I were woven into it on one of the antique looms for making cloth and particularly silk. I am related to many of the people in Angoli, through my grandmother's family, Scalise, and marriages with and into the families of Mazzei, Lucia, Iuliano and others. You will meet some of these "relatives" in later chapters of the book, but for now, suffice it to say that if everyone in Angoli is not related, they certainly act as if they are. With a population of about 300, everyone knows everyone else, and they literally live in very close proximity to one another. Everyone exudes a friendly warmth, and it took no time at all to become part of this culture. My cousins, Sabrina Mazzei and Massimo Uiliano and Rosetta and Carmelo Mazzei make sure that I am introduced to everyone. The families of Angoli are like a large unraveled ball of string, impossible to find the beginning or the end. There are two places in town where I spend a lot of time: the market and coffee bar owned by Carmelo and Rosetta and the restaurant/bar managed by Gaetano Lucia. It is in these two "hangouts" where social interaction springs to life, and the smiles and laughter abound. Everyone is a friend, *"tutti amici."*

As mentioned, Angoli is 13 kilometers or about eight miles by car southeast of Serrastretta, but only much less as the crow flies. It seems much further because the drive takes 20 minutes. To get there on the serpentine road you drive to the top of the mountain above Serrastretta and then half way down the other side. The village is built into a steep hillside, and there are only two parallel streets running horizontally; the upper of the two is the main one with the church and the piazza at the center of its 500-yard length. All the other streets run vertically and are very steep and narrow, some not wide enough for one car and none wide enough for two cars. To walk up is almost impossible for older people, and to walk down is not much easier because you have the sensation you will fall forward. The weather in Angoli is constantly changing; from sunny to cloudy and then sunny again. It could rain lightly at any time when the clouds from the west roll over, and there are times when you are literally in the clouds. You can reach up and touch them; they are below tree top and roof top level.

Many of the homes (P15) in Angoli are hundreds of years old since very few structures are ever raised to ground level. They are simply gutted and refurbished or modernized from the inside out with new plumbing, electrical, gas lines, etc. There is no totally new construction in Angoli. On any given street, most of the houses are attached, almost as if they were cliff dwellings, and the higher up you go, the more spectacular the view. On a clear day, you can see westerly for 30 or more miles (48 kilometers) to the sea and with the sun's reflection planes landing and taking off from the Lamezia International Airport on the coast; and even at times a glimpse Mount Etna rising from Sicily.

Angoli derived its name from the word "triangle." When the village was first settled, on land donated to the peasants by Baroness A'Quino, the location of the first three family homes built formed a triangle with *Crichi Soprano* the point at the top, the old schoolhouse the point on the right and the third the point on the left somewhere near the current town center. The triangle defined the boarders, and the name evolved to become Angoli.

On a bright Sunday in June after mass, I was introduced to Irene Mazzei as people were mingling in the piazza in front of the church. This young, attractive woman spoke no English, but I understood her inviting me to her home that afternoon for coffee at 3:30. I graciously accepted her invitation. Irene lives in *Crichi Soprano,* in the group of homes high above the center of Angoli (P17). I tell more about this story in Chapter XI, and how her 92-year-old grandfather and I traded drink for drink, consuming a variety of fortified beverages.

Calabrians make a wide variety of liqueurs and grappas which are usually enjoyed after a large meal, or socially instead of a coffee; and there are those who add a favorite to coffee. They can produce these digestives out of almost any fruit, herbs and wild plants, and they are said to help the body process foods. Despite their abundance, they are enjoyed in very small portions; and Italians, in general, do not drink alcoholic beverages to excess, but rather in moderation.

On a Sunday morning, just a week before the culmination of the festival of San Giuseppe, I watched as a group of about 10 men of Angoli, ages 40 to 50, erected a large stage in the piazza in front of the church. The stage will be used for entertainment during the final two days of the festival. Once they completed construction, the men adjourned to Gaetano Lucia's restaurant/bar for a sumptuous luncheon complete with wine and linen covered tables. I happened to walk in just as they were finishing, and I was struck by this air of exuberance, this rare combination of excitement and enthusiasm. You could literally feel the emotion and the kinship in the room as the men laughed, joked and sang songs. It was as if they had just conquered the world, and yet this same work is repeated year after year for the festival by probably many of the same men, all in celebration of their patron San Giuseppe. But to these men and the residents of Angoli, this celebration is always new, a renewal of their faith in God, family and their place on earth; and because of these unwavering beliefs, they are completely comfortable with themselves, with who they are and from where they came.

During the summer months around festival time in July, and particularly in August, Angoli swells with visitors. Many are relatives of residents who return to visit parents and grandparents. There are many more people on the street, more children, more cars and parking space is at a premium. The piazza in front of the café/market is crowded with people during the late morning hours as friendships are renewed, relatives are exchanging greetings and fusses are made over a new baby *("bambino")* born since its parents last visited Angoli. Author Karen Haid, an American who taught English in Calabria for more than 10 years, confirmed this observation with the following words: "As is a general trait of the very social Italian people, family ties are extremely close in Calabria. Traditions are still quite strong. Childhood friendships last a lifetime, even when career paths might take classmates in completely different directions. The home village and hometown have meaning, a destination in the mass migration that takes place on holidays and for summer vacations by the Calabrians who have relocated to the north or immigrated to other countries."

The scene is warm, wonderful and filled with laughter. As I mingled among this "family" gathering one morning, I met Maria Cristina Mazzei and her two young sons. Maria is the daughter of Gaetano Mazzei, a retired teacher in Angoli, who now lives near Venice. She is an environmental engineer and her husband is a lawyer. We had a very enlightening conversation, and she took a great interest in the writing of this book, asking me many questions and expressing her opinion on the character of the people.

She believes the people of Serrastretta and its villages are a special breed, and they do not fully understand how unique they are and the values they possess. Now living away, she appreciates it and will pass it on to her children. These villages and the value systems here will survive, she believes.

To Calabrians, and to the people of Serrastretta, life itself is a celebration; and with this conviction, resilience comes naturally. Never is it more apparent or visually obvious than when you witness and participate in the annual festival of San Giuseppe in Angoli (P18,19). The atmosphere is electric with the main street lit from end to end with large lighted arches that flash on and off with thousands of multi-colored flashing bulbs. Hundreds of residents and visitors are walking the main street enjoying food, drink and live entertainment, a three-day party which is barely interrupted by the religious services going on inside the church. All in honor of their patron saint and the celebration of life. Every evening there is live entertainment on the stage, and the café/bar and the restaurant/bar are selling pizzas, grilled sausages and *"panino"* of various kinds about as fast as they can make them. The big day is Sunday beginning at 11:00am with high mass (with the mayor of Serrastretta in attendance), after which everyone goes home for family gatherings and a large mid-day meal. At 6:00pm it starts up again with a two-hour procession complete with the priest, the mayor, the band and many parishioners following behind a dozen men carrying the heavy statue of San Giuseppe. It passes by every home in the village. When they return, the statue is ceremoniously put to bed in the church. More live entertainment, more food and drink, more partying, culminating with a full-scale fireworks display at midnight. The festival is over until next year.

About two weeks after the festival ended, I had just gone into the restaurant/bar for a cocktail when a group of about 10 men assembled at the church, many of the same men who erected the stage. Their task this time was to return the heavy statue of San Giuseppe and Jesus to the large niche high above and behind the alter. I did not go in to watch, but after about 30 minutes they completed their task. And again, they all came into the bar for a refreshment in celebration of their achievement. In mid-August the village held an outdoor spaghetti dinner in honor of the children who decoratively painted a set of steeply ascending steps for the festival (P20,21). Many of the visitors here in August will attend. The quantity of family members who return here in August for their holidays is staggering; there are so many new faces on the street, so many more cars and parking spaces are at a premium. One might think with all these relatives in town Sunday mass would be crowded. Not so. Mass on Sunday, August 12 had the same group of older women in attendance, but no younger couples with children, suggesting further evidence of the Catholic religion's demise in Italy.

In addition to Christmas (P22), there are two other community celebrations in Angoli when all the residents gather. The first is in June when the new piazza in front of the market is transformed into a large dining area. At 7:00pm, hundreds of people enjoy an evening meal together in honor of the first harvests, a dinner consisting mainly of roasted sheep, garden fresh beans and other spring vegetables in various forms, bread, wine and, of course, desert. It ends about 11:00pm. The other festivity is the *"Borgo della Castagna,"* the annual chestnut festival which draws people from the surrounding villages. This year it is scheduled for November 1-3, and at this writing, it is an occasion I look forward to. This I know even in advance: both are demonstrations of Calabrian's indestructible value system based on their beliefs in family, faith and nature, the ingredients for the celebration of life.

Having gone back to the USA for three months, and not returning to Angoli until mid-November, I missed the chestnut festival. But the very first week I was back, the village held a community dinner to thank all those who worked on the festival. It was again an occasion to thank themselves and celebrate their success. My first thought was "I will definitely attend," and my second thought was "What would you expect of the people of Angoli, another excuse for a party." *("Qualsiasi scusa per una festa.")* It is the same with the local soccer team (P23) representing Angoli, Migliuso and Cancello. The players celebrate just as much after a loss as after a victory.

The Sunday afternoon meal was attended by 150 residents and held at the old school which now serves as the parish hall. Again, the men of the parish did the heavy lifting, including most of the food preparation and serving. The meal lasted from 1:00pm until after 5:00pm and included an abundance of food and wine. Even though we ate at long uncovered tables using plastic plates and utensils, it did not detract from the quality of the meal. On the tables was bread, cheese and wine; and the first thing served were individual plates of arborio rice, Milanese style, with bits of salami and fresh hot red peppers to carve and dress the rice if you wanted to swallow fire. Next came individual bowls of minestrone soup made with beans and chopped green vegetables. The broth was outstanding. This was followed by more bread served with grilled, spicy sausages split from end to end. Then more *"carne,"* this time very thinly sliced roasted *"porchetta,"* and more bread. Finally, there was a pause before plates of a variety of fried pastries was served. After this, more deserts of the more sweet *"dolce"* variety and *"gellato."*

The crowning finale was the presentation of a giant inscribed cheese cake (P24) which was paraded around the room. To finish, espresso and grappa. Celebrating life, as no others can.

Life in Angoli always presents me with new surprises and discoveries. It is now one day before Christmas, and I woke up in the middle of the night on December 24th unable to sleep. I went downstairs and fixed myself a cup of hot tea when I heard music playing outside, and then I see a group of people outside my kitchen window. They were singing Christmas songs, and then began yelling my name, so I opened my door and greeted everyone in this group of about eight young adults. They were playing a variety of musical instruments, hastily assembled, and were filled with the joy of Christmas. Earlier in the evening when I was at the pub, I commented to Gaetch that I was disappointed the large cut Christmas tree was still laying on the ground, not up and decorated yet. He said maybe tomorrow. Again, however, I witnessed a celebration of villagers, and their expression of happiness is beautiful to witness.

It was now later in the day on Christmas Eve, and I ate alone then fell asleep at 7:00pm. I awoke at 11:00pm and prepared to go to midnight mass, followed by the lighting of the bonfire in the piazza in front of the market. It was cold and rainy, but that did not seem to deter any of the villagers from assembling. The fire was lit to the cheers of those gathered, and it was expressions of *"Buon Natale"* to everyone around. I then went to the pub for a Christmas grappa with Gaetch, and finally retired at 2:30am. The Christmas holiday officially ends on January 8, and Italy may be the only country where a holiday is declared to end a holiday. I happened to be in Serrastretta on January 8, and I was surprised to observe all the businesses were closed, even the cafes.

The Village of Cancello

My first venture away from Angoli to one of the other villages was to Cancello about three miles (five kilometers) away to the south down the mountain. The first thing you notice is a stark contrast with Angoli because the main street is much wider and even has parking spaces curbside in the center of town. You are also struck by Cancello's much more modern appearance. The homes look newer, larger and more well maintained, and they are not clustered or attached as in Angoli. I made two visits there, the first looking for a recommended restaurant with excellent pizza. I did not find it, then later discovered it in the very center of town at the main intersection across the street from the church; a church which is much smaller and looks to be no more than 50 years old. On this first visit to Cancello, I went into a coffee bar and a general store where I even made a purchase. I noticed the people I interacted with seemed rather somber and did not engage in any small talk that you would expect as a customer, but I did not think much of it until my second visit.

I went back to Cancello the following day and was determined to have pizza for lunch at the recommended restaurant Top Country. As I was approaching, the owner walked by me staring me down as if I was from another planet, while all this time I thought I blended in quite well. I entered and immediately ordered a beer to establish myself as a customer, and then looked around at the very handsome surroundings. It had a very ample wine section with a good selection of both local and Tuscan wines, some rather high priced. There were two dining rooms separated from the bar and shop areas, one downstairs and one upstairs. I then ordered two pieces of pizza and another beer and took my food outside to eat on the terrace. At no time during my hour there did the owner or his wife speak to me with a simple *"ciao," "grazi,"* or *"arrivederci"* as I paid and left. I was told later that Cancello was an offshoot of Angoli, the reason for its newer appearance and no centuries old looking structures. Assuming this to be true, those who first went there certainly did not transport the *"tutti amici"* culture with them.

Not satisfied with my own quickly formed opinion and determined to learn more, I went back a third time and stopped into a different bar/restaurant/ night club that was open at mid-day. The young owner of Café Sunset was extremely outgoing and introduced himself as Simone Lucia. Did you ever wonder why bars are often the most-friendly places? It is no surprise they are social gathering places, regardless of the country you are in, and it is where you go when you usually want to talk; you walk in and say "Set'em up Giuseppe." I asked Simone where the *Panificio San Georgio* (the local commercial bread bakery) was located, and he took the time to escort me there. My curiosity about bread making was the reason I went back to Cancello this third time and I was hopeful to see the operation in production. Naturally, bread is made during the night time hours, so it is ready for delivery first thing in the morning; and this particular bakery supplied all the markets in the surrounding villages. The owner's wife greeted us and said we should come back for a tour at 2:00am.

Simone (P25) invited me to his bar for dinner at 9:00pm, after which we will go to the bakery. My immediate thought was how this will be a test of my physical resilience. As luck would have it, we did not go on the 2:00am bakery tour for what reason I could not be sure, except Simone said he would rather I see his mother make bread the way it has always been done in a wood fired domed oven (P26). Despite not seeing the bakery in production, our dinner conversation was lively and animated. Simone is a man in love with American nostalgia and the ambience of his establishment totally reflect this. The place is filled with eclectic memorabilia, album covers, posters, pictures, signs and trinkets from 30 to 50 years ago. Consistent with this, he still likes to take photos with an old Poloroid camera even though the quality is very poor compared with today's digital images.

When we were near the end of our meal, a large group of his family members came in, including babies; and I was introduced to everyone. The family bonding lit up the room. When things quieted down we continued to talk, and I realized that here was another local small business owner who loves life, works hard and has no fear of the future. Simone, like the others, knows full well that populations are dwindling because many of his contemporaries leave for university educations and jobs, but they are not overly concerned or worried about it. Their undying faith in the future tells them *"Quello che sara, sara"* (what will be, will be); and it is this character strength, this resilience, that carries them forward. For reasons they best appreciate, they comfortably know and accept that the short span of their life is a gift rooted in centuries old traditions of generations long past. This treasured gift of life they will pass on to new generations, and they find peace and comfort in so doing.

Ironically, I ran into Don Emmanuel several times during these daily visits to Cancello because he was in Angoli every day during the week immediately preceding the culmination of the festival. We had the opportunity, therefore, to discuss the opposing point of view that in the end is not opposed at all. We decided in our discussions that we are both correct. Yes, the population of the villages will diminish; and, yes, those who stay will insure that the traditions and values continue. Again, the resilience of the Calabrian people will be called upon, possibly in ways never previously experienced. This time the threat comes from within. Those who leave will probably not come back, and those who stay may be called upon to persevere and adapt in ways not yet imagined.

The Village of Migliuso

The village of Migliuso, just half way between Angoli and Cancello, has a much older appearance, not unlike Angoli, except it is built more vertically up and down a gently sloping hillside. The main café/bar and market is immediately behind the church. It carries the family name, Bar Emporio Cianflone and is run by a father and son (P27) with one employee in the market section. The son, Alessio Cianflone, understands very well that the business is his to run once his father retires; and not only is he resigned to this future, he relishes it. The family also has two daughters, both in Rome attending university, one in engineering and the other in architecture. Neither plan to return to Migliuso, but Alessio who is 30 and single will stay. Alessio has become a good friend and my "banker." He exchanges the cash I need against a charge on my Social Security debit card, and he does so without charging me a transaction fee, whereas at the Angoli market, I am charged 3.50 Euro. Even better, the Emporio Cianflone has a greater variety of merchandise and is better stocked.

When trying to question Alessio on why he will stay, the answers may be so simple they are difficult to express; or the answer to him is so obvious, the question is a stupid one. His answer came forward in two words: friendly and hospitable, unlike the big cities of northern Italy. He places the most importance on being together with the people he loves, the family, and he avoids addressing the issue of young people moving away for an education and jobs as if to say there will be enough people who will find value in what Calabria has to offer, its mountains, its seashore and its food. In the end, this may prove to be a shortsighted viewpoint, but he is a cheerful, happy young man with a very positive attitude. After all, he concluded, Calabrians ability to persevere, adapt and survive comes directly from their stubbornness and their pride.

The Village of Accaria

One day on the way to Nicastro, I passed through Accaria and decided to stop for a coffee at one of the two cafes. I sat out front enjoying my coffee and during the next half-hour at least 12 customers arrived for socializing; but no one spoke to me, nor did I make any attempt to engage anyone in conversation. I decided to do that on a second visit there. I did, however, drive around the village. It is quite spread out as if wrapped around the curvature of a steep hillside. When viewed from different points of the curvature, it resembles a necklace of tiny strung together hamlets, each with 10 to 20 homes. Each of the hamlets has a sub-name such as Rosario Accaria. There is a cemetery situated in the center, and there are two churches, one at each end of town.

I have driven through Accaria quite a few times, but one day I decided to stop and make a concerted effort to engage some residents in conversation. After parking the car on the main street in the center of town, I went into the Fox Bar and Café shortly before lunch time. I ordered a *"caffee Americano,"* and asked the woman who served me if anyone might be coming in who speaks English. After using the translation app on my cell phone, her response was "no." So, I enjoyed my coffee and waited. Within 10 minutes, a young woman entered and stood at the bar next to me. I immediately engaged her in conversation and offered to buy her coffee. She said she spoke very little English, but after I explained my reason for being in the bar, she became more talkative and was willing to answer some of my questions.

Then a man entered who she greeted, and he then became part of the conversation. She told me her name is Gabriella Scicchitano, age 27, and works as a shop assistant nearby. As the conversation continued, her English improved; she and the man, Rosario Gallo (P28), collaborated on the answers to my questions. At one point, he told me his mother was a Scalise. They told me the population of Accaria is 400; and when I raised the issue of why there are two churches in town, they spoke up with pride, saying the old church, at the other end of town, was too small. Now Accaria has two *"Chiesa dell'Immacolata."*

I explained to them about this book and its title. We talked about the resilience of the Calabrian people, and they were quick to use the words "strong" and "humble" as defining their character; but the strongest characteristics, they agreed, was "working together" and "winners." *("lavorare insieme e vincente").*

The Village of San Michele

I drove through the village of San Michele several times and was struck by its appearance of being deserted. There was no activity, no people on the streets, no old men sitting on benches and no café/bar that I could find. It caused me to wonder if San Michele will be the first of the Serrastretta villages to be completely abandoned. Only time will tell. On my second visit to San Michele, I noticed two men sitting on a park bench just as I entered the village. I stopped the car, got out and approached them in the hope of having a conversation. Of course, neither one spoke English, but one of them was willing to attempt a conversation. He was Mario Fazio, and with the help of the translation app on my cell phone, we were able to communicate, although barely. He told me the village has only 80 residents and the number continues to decline. He holds on to a belief the village will survive.

I asked him about the location of the Benedictine *"Monastero della Resurrezione,"* said to be located in San Michelle. He pointed down the main street, and as he was doing so, Roberto Talarico from Angoli pulled up in his car. I asked him about the monastery and got a similar response. Both men explained to me in Italian that the monastery is only open at Christmas, and I took this to mean open to the public. Mario then escorted me to the monastery and walked me around the property. On the way back to my car, I noticed a tobacco shop, so I peered in from the doorway. It was a very tiny establishment with a few shelves for grocery items. You might say it was fitting for a village with only 80 residents. I found out later the monastery never did open at Christmas, and it is unoccupied the majority of the time; and run by the Order of Saint Benedict from another Benedictine monastery in Greece.

There are hundreds of villages in the Calabrian mountains like those of *"Comune di Serrastretta"* with populations under 500. Each has its own story to tell, its own history and traditions; but their commonality is the character of the people, their love for each other and the foundation of their values rooted in family, faith and nature…their resilience.

CHAPTER IV:

The Popular Priest, The Remarkable Rabbi, And The Marvelous Mayor

(La Sacerdote Popalare, Il Notevole Rabbino, E Il Magnifico Sindaco)

"To be filled with life, its precious gifts;
Then leave your mark upon the earth."
— *The Author*
From "The Art Of Living"

One morning while I was sitting at the Gallo Pasticceria enjoying a *"caffee Americano"* and a pastry, someone said to me there is a man here you should meet who speaks very good English. I was introduced to Gaspare Mancuso, and when he first spoke I was dumbfounded to hear English with no trace of an Italian accent; his mannerisms and speech were so American, I immediately thought he must be in Serrastretta on vacation, but I also heard him speak Italian to others near-by. Our conversation was enlightening as he explained that he was born in Serrastretta, holds dual citizenship and lives in Texas, but spends the spring and summer months here where his brother still lives. Having moved to the United States at a very young age, he received all his education in America and is now retired after a full professional career in Texas.

Without any hesitation, he emphatically said Serrastretta is the best place in the world to live. "There is nowhere in the United States that can match what you have here," he told me; and his explanation of why this is so was very telling. He went on to elaborate by saying to me, "Where else could you live surrounded by such natural beauty where everyone is friendly and happy, where you can get to know everyone, and where anxiety and the rat race don't exist?"

Why tell this story while leading into a chapter about a local priest, rabbi and mayor? The three people to whom this chapter is devoted are a big part of the reason for Gasper's feelings. As community leaders, Don Luigi Iuliano, Rabbi Barbara Aiello and Mayor Felice Molinaro help create and perpetuate the environment which is Serrastretta and its villages. They are totally devoted to what they do, they understand and are comfortable with the role they play, and the people of Serrastretta love them for it.

Don Luigi Iluiano, pastor emeritus of the Serrastretta parish and pastor of the Church of Carmine *(Chiesa del Carmine)* in Lamezia Terme may be the best known individual in the entire area surrounding Serrastretta. As mentioned earlier, he is known to everyone as Don Gigi; and I was fortunate enough to live in his home for three weeks. I got to know him and understand him quite well despite his lack of English and my poor beginner's Italian. He lives in this grand house about four kilometers outside of town. I described the house in the previous chapter, but suffice it to say that the house and its large property are Don Gigi's domain, his castle, his palace, his fortress, his passion, and he is dedicated to it in the extreme. This obsession he has calls to mind the admonition of Leonardo da Vinci: "Never take unto yourself something you cannot do without."

The Popular Priest

I have already written quite a bit about Don Guiseppe Uiliano (Don Gigi) (P29) in Chapter II, but those observations were based on my living in his home for three weeks without the benefit of any meaningful conversation with him. But now, I have conducted a complete interview with him using the assistance of a translator. It took quite a few attempts to get him to schedule the interview, and even though I drove past his house many times on the back and forth to Serrastretta, he was either not at home or delayed setting a schedule. He always seemed happy to see me, and always offered me a coffee when I walked in.

The one thing I immediately noticed after returning from three months in the US, was he continues to make improvements on his beautiful home. He enclosed the walkway between the main house and the private chapel behind. The wall on the left side is now glassed-in with a huge stained-glass window, I believe depicting Santa Maria del Soccorso from the church in Serrastretta. And as always, you can be sure the house is pristine and very well maintained. Don Gigi told me during the interview he has spent the last 20 years on renovations

Luigi Iuliano is a true local, born in Serrastretta in 1954; his parents are Giuseppe and Rosa, and he has one sister, Maria. He was educated in classical theology, and considers himself a true conservative. In no way does he see the Catholic Church changing, and he believes it will survive as it always has, because, he says, it was founded by the Holy Spirit. I got the distinct impression he views the church within himself, and when you ask him why he became a priest, he credits "A devine calling." In response to my specific question on why men in Italy generally do not attend church, his response was, "They believe they can live without God." Possibly you can discern by the way I have written Don Gigi's comments, that in conversation, he is very direct and emphatic.

We spent some time talking about the character of the "mountain people" and Calabrians in general, and he used the words "family," "friendship" and "solidarity" repeatedly; and he went on about how the locale and the environment determine the character and personality of the people. "Our warmth and hospitality define us," he said with an air of pride. Don Gigi capped off his remarks by telling me the peaceful surroundings of Serrastretta, with its clean air and water, create a relaxing, meditative environment away from the chaos of the city.

After we finished the interview, and as I was driving away, I wondered why Don Gigi has achieved such local popularity and notoriety, and even though he is one of the few here I know as well, I struggled for an answer. Ten minutes later when I arrived back in Angoli, I came up with an answer. Don Luigi Iuliano is a man

of very strong convictions who is not bashful about expressing his opinions; and people respect him for this
even though they may not agree. When you possess
this personality trait, it does not hurt being a priest. He
combines this with his generosity and the use of his
beautiful home, expressing his generosity through en-
tertaining. When I asked Mayor Felice Molinaro about
Don Gigi's popularity, he shared with me his tribute
to the local priest when Don Gigi was assigned to his
parish in Lamezia Terme. He said, "We appreciated the
charm of your strong personality, enriched and multi-
faceted culture and your brilliant experiences; the great
charisma that you transmit in your homilies, with the
unmistakable emphasis that characterizes them."

The Remarkable Rabbi

I first met Rabbi Barbara Aiello (P30) in 2015 when
my cousin Susan Bevevino and I were doing some family ancestral research in preparation for the first Bevevino
family reunion since 1988. We ran across her name on
the internet and started reading about her, discovering,
of all things, that she was born in Pittsburgh, Pennsylvania, not far from where I grew up (just outside Butler,
PA about 40 miles north of Pittsburgh). Rabbi Barbara
is, however, now located in Serrastretta, the ancestral
home of her family. Her grandparents and parents were
born in Serrastretta, then moved to Pittsburgh in 1920.
As she was growing up she became intrigued with her
Jewish religion and her roots. She studied to become a
rabbi and eventually moved to Serrastretta, and now has
a synagogue there. She is the first female rabbi in Italy
and is considered the leading authority on the Jewish

roots of Calabrians. During our own Bevevino/Scalise family investigation in 2015 just prior to a family reunion, Rabbi Barbara was most helpful in giving us some leads that filled in pieces to the Bevevino family puzzle.

Rabbi Barbara's synagogue is named Ner Tamid del Sud (The Eternal Light of the South) and is the first active synagogue in Calabria in 500 years. She says with pride, "As rabbi and founder, it is a joy and a challenge for me to work here, especially since Serrastretta is the village where my father was raised and where Jews settled and practiced in secret for over 400 years." She fully appreciates and honors the fact that Serrastretta's founders were Jewish families forced out of Sicily, but virtually all converted to Catholicism, adapted and thus survived. Her own family hung onto its original beliefs; and it was her grandmother, Felicia Scalise, who centuries later maintained the remnants of Jewish practices and passed them on. After moving to Pittsburgh, Rabbi Barbara's own grandmother held onto her Jewish traditions. On her very first Friday night in Pittsburgh, "...she gathered up her candles, challah and wine and headed downstairs. My father stopped her at the cellar door. He said, 'Mama, you're in America now, the land of the free and the home of the brave!' But she pushed him aside and continued on saying 'You can't be too sure!'"

While telling these stories of preserving Jewish traditions here in Serrastretta, Rabbi Barbara concluded, "For centuries we Calabrians took our Jewish traditions into our homes and our hearts and slowly, at first for safety reasons, and then for cultural reasons, the religious meanings of these rituals were lost. Our precious Jewish customs became family traditions, nothing more." There is no doubt that she is on a mission, one that will carry her forward for the rest of her life. Her Calabrian synagogue and the Jewish Cultural Center, which she also started, "… creates a traditional complement for the religious experience, allows Italians and Italian-Americans to explore their Jewish traditions in an atmosphere of warmth and welcome."

My first face to face meeting with Rabbi Barbara was in Serrastretta just a few weeks after first arriving, and now I bump into her regularly on the street where we engage in casual conversation. We have, however, set a time for a more serious discussion on her views about the Calabrian people's resilience. We sat down for an in-depth hour and a half conversation at the Gallo Pasticceria and she shared with me many of her views on southern Italy, Calabria, Serrastretta and her work to restore Judaism here and uncover its past. According to Rabbi Barbara, Judaism died in southern Italy 500 years ago despite the fact many of the people who first settled here from Sicily were Jewish, as my ancestors were. Its revival, if it ever happens, is a slow tedious process. She has been in Serrastretta full time for 15 years, and was coming to Calabria regularly before that. True, she has the first active synagogue in southern Italy in 500 years, but her congregation numbers only 82. Even more unique, the 82 members come from all over southern Italy and as far away as Naples.

Rabbi Barbara travels a great deal because she is often called upon to conduct Jewish ceremonies (weddings, bar and bat mitsvas, conversions, etc.) all over Calabria and the other southern regions. She will tell you that it is not her role to convert Catholics back to

Judaism, for she is not a missionary (the Jewish religion has none) but her role is to uncover the Jewish past here and share what she finds with those who are interested in knowing more about their roots. This, she believes, is her greatest accomplishment as a rabbi, no matter how slow the progress.

One of the worst periods for Italian Jews, and even for some Catholics who maintained some Jewish traditions, was the occupation by the Germans during the Second World War. Again, Jews went into hiding, and what Jewish symbolism did exist, whether Jewish or Catholic, was hidden or disguised. Some of the symbolism is here in Serrastretta today, and some here remains hidden. She told me the story of how her husband was an identical twin, and as a small child growing up Jewish in Italy was a target for German experimentation; but he and his brother were saved by a Catholic priest who provided them false identity documents.

I asked Rabbi Barbara how she would define resilience, and her answer was simple and direct. She said, "Always moving forward; courage and hope in the future." It immediately struck me how these words constitute a complete reflection of how the people of Serrastretta view their religious faith and their unwavering attachment to their patron saint, the Blessed Virgin Mary of Perpetual Help. Calabrians, she said, are survivors because they know how to make the best of bad situations. With current unemployment at 27 percent, they not only survive, but thrive. Bartering is a way of life in Calabria, and the people know how to provide for themselves and their families by trading one service for another or one commodity for another. By no stretch of the imagination are they *"terrones,"* a derogatory term meaning "dumb peasant" often used in the north to describe southern Italians. To Rabbi Barbara, possibly one of the best examples of resilience, "...courage and hope in the future," was the migration of Calabrians to North America between 1880 and 1920. Her family and mine are testimony to this.

We concluded our enriching conversation with Rabbi Barbara expressing her hope for the future. Yes, she believes the villages in Calabria will continue to decline in population as some have even disappeared completely, leaving a small complex of homes and shops without residents. These empty shells will not be re-inhabited, but where villages do survive, as is the case for Serrastretta, its traditions, its culture, its character will move it forward. Serrastretta is resilient.

The Marvelous Mayor

Before I arrived in Calabria, I made several attempts to reach Serrastretta's Mayor Felice Molinaro (P31) by email, but with no success. He did not respond. I took it upon myself, after enjoying a cappuccino and pastry at the Gallo Pasticceria, to venture into City Hall and attempt to see the mayor without an appointment. I introduced myself at reception and then to the mayor's executive assistant; after which I was escorted to a waiting area immediately outside his office, asked to wait and told he would be here in 10 minutes. He arrived on time, and we went into his office. A cordial, informal discussion began, and I realized he was not surprised to see me; and his English was better than I expected. He was a little pressed for time, but we made an appointment for the following week. The best news I received from him was the fact he had read the prospectus on this book and he was pleased and excited about its subject matter. We ended our first meeting in about 15 minutes, after he told me I would have his complete cooperation for this project.

Our second meeting a week later was also rather hurried because, he said, there were some very pressing community issues he had to deal with. However, we did have enough time to arrive at a full understanding of my needs, i.e. interviewing him for the book to learn his views on the character of Serrastretta's residents, and some questions I had about my own family's history here. He told me he could also help with my need to secure a long-term visa to complete my work. Then he asked that I send him two separate emails with my needs and questions in detail.

Several months went by without completing the interview, but I did see him on a number of occasions. Finally, the day arrived for the detailed interview. My impression of him from our times together is Mayor *("sindaco")* Molinaro is a very polished, complete gentleman, and a true politician with the ability to speak clearly and precisely in Italian, and even in English. He is a graduate of the University of Bologna with a degree in engineering. He was first elected mayor in 2011 winning 62 percent of the vote. He was re-elected in 2016 with 92 percent of the vote. He must have done something right.

I remember him telling me during our first meeting eight months earlier that he believed the people of Serrastretta epitomized resilience, which I was happy to hear, but I questioned if it was just the politician talking.

Now I can say it was not. Even more interesting to me was his unsolicited comment that the people of Angoli represented the best example of resilience because they exhibit the greatest amount of community spirit. They are all one and express their joy of life as one as if they were a single family.

Mayor Molinaro put a great amount of thought into our interview, so much so that he laboriously wrote, in Italian and English, some parting words to give me. When I was last sitting in his office to receive them, he was still editing the copy being the perfectionist he is. When he finally finished, I jokingly asked him if he was trying to make it perfect. The only way I can do his brief text full justice is to quote it completely:

"Angoli is an evolved and modern village, albeit from the ancient heart, and the people, despite the progress, the education and the inevitable contaminations that the evolution of civilization brings with it, in the principles and in the heart, it is that of the past. As a mayor, I am deeply proud of our people, of the values that characterize our community, as well as the beauties that the Creator has given to this territory: a village immersed in the green hills but majestically overlooking the sea, a small village that in its simplicity and beauty, almost seems like a crib. But I am sure that more than our peculiarities, the excellence and the amenity of this area of Calabria, what certainly remains impressed in the heart and memories of visitors is the people."

"Angoli is an integral and cohesive community, characterized by a great sense of identity and belonging; it is made up of good people, honest, hardworking, enterprising and accustomed to sacrifice, generous and hospitable people. People who respect the moral and social norms, fearful of God and His commandments. Men and women who believe in the value of the family, as a foundation of God's community and plan on earth, in friendship, solidarity and respect for others. People who believe that work, starting from that of the earth, is not only a means to obtain a living, but is really an instrument that ennobles man, who through his sacrifices and the sweat of his brow makes himself worthy of respect of the Lord, and feels in harmony with himself and with the Creator."

"I believe that the resilience of Angoli and its people is grounded in these characteristics, in these values and in these sentiments."

You have just met three unique community leaders, each with a different background, but all three in love with Serrastretta and totally dedicated to its preservation. They are true local heroes.

CHAPTER V

Meet The Young People Of Resilience

(Incontra I Giovani Di Resilenza)

"Polio's dream around 80 BC, but
son of da Vinci after fifteen centuries.
In harmony, at peace with the universe;
you are the symbol of our humanity.
Ageless forever is your destiny;
your eyes gaze at us, as it should be."

— The Author
From "Son Of da Vinci"
(The Vitruvian Man)

Some of the first people I talked with, and eventually interviewed, were the young people of Serrastretta and its villages, from 18 to mid-30ies in age. It literally took me aback after showing some of them a picture of Leonardo da Vinci, most did not know who it was. Here was a picture of the greatest genius ever to live and obviously the greatest and most famous Italian, and he was not recognized. This must be a shortcoming of the Italian education system. However, maybe not a surprise. Many Americans in the same age group probably cannot recognize a picture of George Washington.

Defining Their Own Success at Home

I sat down with two young men, Andrea Caruso, age 31, and Filippo Talarico, age 22, for a discussion about the resilience of the Serrastretta people. Andrea is a supervisor at the Lamezia Terme airport, having started his job there seven years ago, working his way up from baggage handler, to ramp agent and now to a supervisory position. He did not attended a university, but did spend a few years in Australia where he learned his English. He wants to stay in Serrastretta and raise a family. Filippo is an aspiring fashion designer, but still living at home supported by his parents. He wants to make his way to Milan and pursue his career there, but eventually come back to raise a family. He uses traditional Calabrian costumes of old for his inspiration and dress designs.

Both young men profess to be atheists (better stated as agnostic) mainly because they are disillusioned, not so much with religion, but by the Catholic Church; and yet they maintain a strong belief in family and tradition. I have seen this same attitude expressed by my 26-year-old son-in-law. It struck me that Andrea and Filippo both brought up nature, and how close they feel to it being from Serrastretta. They fully appreciate "working the soil;" and they expressed it this way: "We understand that an apple comes from a tree, not from the supermarket." Their families have taught them this belief in nature, mostly by example. Filippo's last name tells me he is descendant from one of the five founding families of Serrastretta, yet he knowns little of his family history or Serrastretta history.

Their disillusionment with the Catholic Church is, for the most part, based on what they consider abusive power and control, greed and a lack of true concern for the underprivileged. It has nothing to do with pedophilia scandals. They view the Catholic Church as corrupt, and no different or better than the Mafia. Both young men know Don Gigi and Rabbi Barbara, and their opinions about Don Gigi are consistent with mine, as previously expressed; and they see very little or no presence of Judaism in Serrastretta. They are fully aware of the Mafia's presence, not in Serrastretta, but in Lamezia. It has a very real dominance here, and according to Andrea and Filippo it simply blends into the landscape. Those involved in the Mafia lead common, everyday lives just like everyone else. Nothing major gets done in Calabria, they say, without the approval and involvement of the Mafia and the Church.

We talked about northern verses southern Italian attitudes, and they were quick to point out the differences, or what they believe is a vast divide. Southern Italians are referred to as *"terroni,"* or "to live for life;" while northern Italians are known as *"polentone,"* meaning "to live for work." And yet there is an irony here. Northern Italians come south for their inexpensive holidays, while southern Italians go north for better jobs and are well regarded for their work ethic.

Both Andrea and Pilippo were most willing to openly express their views, and they enjoyed several marijuana smokes during our discussion, proudly telling me they grow their own only for private use. We concluded our discussion with both young men expressing the belief that Serrastretta will continue and survive much the way it is. Why? The answer is simple. The people here "live for life," and there will always be those Italians who treasure and seek this.

The meeting with Andrea and Filippo was just the first in a series I held with small groups of young people from Serrastretta.

The public education system offered in southern Italy may not match the quality of northern Italy's. However, the young people of Serrastretta most definitely have aspirations that reach beyond Calabria, yet they remain part of its fabric; they will always return, if not in person, in spirit. They will always "live for life."

Dedicated to Success in Calabria

I continue to be impressed and encouraged by the young people I meet in Calabria; you can sense their desires, aspirations and even their fearlessness when it comes to hard work. Their work ethic is readily apparent. I took the opportunity one Saturday to venture outside the Serrastretta area to the town of Decollatura in search of the monastery where I spent one night the first week I was in Calabria. I stopped at a Bar Liceo at the far edge of town in the hope I might engage in conversation and aid my search. I met a young man who turned out to be the owner's son and he spoke enough English to understand what I was looking for. He ended up being much more helpful than I could imagine, telephoning the monastery to get directions and even escorting me there on a trial run. We had time since it was only 10:00am and I was invited for lunch at noon.

Because of our time together in the car and at the bar, I conducted a casual interview, much like the discussion with Andrea and Filippo.

The young man is Georgio Indresso, a bright 25-year-old who has returned home from Milan where he studied visual design and graphics. His desire is to build his career in Calabria and in his hometown, knowing that one day he will be called upon to also run the family business. He loves the local atmosphere, the warmth of family, open space and fresh air. He even mentioned his love for the local food as a reason to stay, yet he is committed to success in his chosen professional career. Is this a young man who wants the best of both worlds? Maybe so, but I would bet he will be successful. After all, he is a Calabrian whose resilience will propel him forward. One might think it would be the older generations who best understand and can define or explain the secrets to their resilience, but so far, I have found that it is the younger people who best express how and why it is so deeply rooted here. I may be wrong in this preliminary assessment, and further investigation will tell me, but the young people get it; and whether they choose to leave or stay, this gift will remain with them.

If, in fact, life is a celebration and considered the greatest of gifts, then you can understand why Calabrians both young and old, are always happy, always smiling, always warm and friendly, and always pleased to say *"buon giorno."* To act otherwise would demonstrate they have no appreciation for the gift of life.

Studying Law at a Distant University But "Home is Home"

During the summer months, and particularly in August, Serrastretta, Angoli and other towns in Calabria swell with visiting relatives, back home to see their parents and grandparents. One late afternoon while I was standing along the main street in Angoli (near my WiFi access) trying to make calls to the United States, a young man approached, stopped and seemed as if he wanted to chat. He introduced himself as Eugenio Gallo from the Como area and he was in town with his parents to visit his grandparents. He was curious why I was in Angoli, and as I explained my situation, he became very interested in my family story telling me he would ask his family about possible connections to my grandfather.

The following day Eugenio and I met again, so I took the opportunity to garner his thoughts on resilience. He was eager to express himself, being a fourth-year law student at the University of Insubria in Verese. He believes those who leave here take their Calabrian values and strengths with them. "Home is home," he said, and returning here will always be a goal for his future family. He told me about visits his grandparents made to Como from their home in Angoli. "Their eyes say it when they are away. The light is gone," said Eugenio.

Some Will Stay and Some Will Go

At the restaurant/bar in Angoli where I spend a lot of time, there are two young women who work there in the summer months, and I have gotten to know them quite well. They always seem happy to see me which has nothing to do with me, but rather with their character trait of treating everyone as friend and family. Miriam Mascaro is 18 and lives in Migliuso, the Serrastretta village just a few kilometers away. She is about to begin her last year of high school, and then will go to a local university where she wants to study physical therapy. Her desire is to move away and hopefully go to America. My other *"amica"* is Maria Francesca DeSantis from Angoli, a 20-year-old student at the University of Calabria, majoring in tourism science. She is about to leave for six months of study in Spain, an exchange program which is part of her degree requirement. I asked her, "Why tourism science?" She quickly responded that she will stay in Calabria, and probably Angoli, because her goal is to make Calabria a better place for tourism and share with others it traditions, its food and its friendly people.

To Miriam and Maria (P32), resilience boils down to living every day with a good attitude and being honest with family and friends. Their term for the celebration of life is *"celabrazione di vita,"* or even better stated they said, *"vivi la vita."* Live the life.

Making the Choice for Place and Family

In Calabria there is a chain of small markets or grocery stores that specialize in locating in the smaller villages; and one such market is in Serrastretta. The name of the chain is Puntoe Market, and there are more than 70 of them. The one in Serrastretta is staffed by young women who are very helpful and customer conscious. The senior member of the team is Elisabetta Fazio (P33), a woman in her mid-thirties with two young sons, ages 11 and seven. She graduated from the University of Calabria with a degree in tourism, but then found it impossible to both stay in Serrastretta and pursue a career in her field. She has been working at the market for 16 years.

She had to make a choice; and it was to stay because of her love for Serrastretta, its people, its culture and her family. Elisabetta observed, quite correctly, it takes courage to stay and courage to leave. Her attitude about many young people leaving comes down to a belief that those who stay will find new ways to help Serrastretta thrive, and she is committed to doing her part. Yet, she understands that in the process the villages will shrink, but they will survive. She does not view the situation as a negative, but rather as an opportunity. It does no good, she told me, to be saddened by a situation you cannot prevent.

They Are The Future

Meet newlyweds Cristian Iuliano and Alessia Della Porta, married in the Angoli's church of San Giuseppe just three days before I interviewed them, and the evening before they were leaving on their honeymoon to South America. When they return, they will live in Torino in the north of Italy. Cristian, 35, is from Migliuso, and Alessia, 30, from Angoli. To Cristian and Alessia (P34), Torino allows them to grow, to be more open and have a bigger vision of life. But to them, Calabria is home, and they, like the others who have moved away, cannot imagine Calabria losing its way of life or its traditions.

They talked about the wedding guests who came from far distances and foreign countries: Spain, Portugal, Greece, and how impressed they were with Calabrian values of family, friendship and a genuine caring for one another, not to mention the food. I was privileged to eat, drink and converse with these guests, all of whom were very impressive young adults. It is no accident that the newlyweds have these quality young people as friends.

Cristian, Alessia and I talked about resilience, and they had some unique ways of defining it. For them, some of the keys are resistance to domination and the willingness to always sacrifice for family. The people of Calabria will not allow the destruction of their way of life and their traditions. They also understand, however, that the young are changing and exist with a newer mentality which may erode the cherished values in Calabria. I came away from the interview believing very strongly that Cristian and Alessia are the future of Calabria, whether they return or not. For certain, they will pass the values on to their future children.

A Young Man Strives Pursuing Two Careers

I was at the bar in the restaurant early one evening, when in walked a young man with a full head of red hair and a red beard. I had never seen him before, but we exchanged greetings and I introduced myself. He told me his name is Danilo Scalise (P35) and he was aware of my work in Angoli. I was taken by the red hair and now realized this genetic trait is present in the Scalise family, even showing up in some of my Bevevino relatives in the United States. His family in Angoli has a few members with red hair, Fabio Lucia and Giuseppe Scalise, to name just two. His father is Antonio Scalise and his mother Lucia Maria Franca, living in Angoli.

Danilo and I had a very good conversation, in part because he was proficient in English, but it was for other more meaningful reasons. He told me he lives in Milan and pursues two careers, as a musician and as an electrical engineer. His passion is playing the piano, and you could not help but feel he is a true artist. He studied at the Milan Conservatory of Music, and learned his engineering skills in technical school. Now at age 33, he is married and has a three-month-old child. I observed him to be extremely intelligent as he exhibited a great knowledge of Italian history and the origins of the Calabrian people; and he fully understood the significance of tradition and the role of family, faith and nature. To Danilo, resilience comes down to the capacity to overcome limits placed upon you, even when they are the result of dramatic events.

We parted company after about 30 minutes of conversation, and I could not help but feel I had just met someone I would like to spend more time with.

Much In Common, Even Our Name

There is a beautiful young woman, 31, who is from outside the Serrastretta area, and it just so happens we share the same surname. Both with the name Bevivino (Bevevino), it goes far beyond a random coincidence, which you will discover more about in the last chapter of this book. Her name in Rossana Bevivino (P36) from Tiriolo, a town of 3000 residents about 20 kilometers east of Serrastretta.

Rossana is well educated, speaks fluent English and works for a supermarket supply company as a marketing analyst. She received her higher education at the University of Calabria in engineering. She is married to Antonio Concolino who works locally in the funeral supply business, and the couple have a two-year-old boy named Leonardo. This young family is committed to staying in Calabria, knowing there are much better job opportunities in the large northern cities. Regardless of where you live, she believes, life is filled with opportunity and risk, so people must adapt, and the people of Calabria are born with this characteristic. "We Calabrians are very clever at creating new ideas and finding ways to survive," she told me.

A Firm Belief in his Ancient Roots

During the winter months when Angoli is quiet and not filled with visitors and tourists, the restaurant in town is only open four evenings a week, Thursday through Sunday. It does not provide much in the way of job opportunities, and Gaetano Lucia, the manager, is on some days required to operate the pub by himself; but on most winter evenings, he has a young chef from Accaria in the kitchen. He is 19-year-old Luca Fragale (P37) who is quite accomplished given his young years. His hometown of Accaria is where his parents are, and he is committed to stay, because to Luca "family comes first."

He wants to build his career in food service locally and stay in Calabria forever. Luca told me during one of our many conversations at the pub, that the people of Serrastretta and its villages are "very open-hearted and welcoming." He credits history and the area's historic past for the wonderful character of Calabrians and its mountain people. "Our strength of character, our resilience," he believes, "comes from ancient people." Luca concluded our conversation with these words: "We can adapt to anything, and we know how to survive."

After speaking with all the young people featured in this chapter, and getting to know many of them quite well, I am convinced they will carry on (and pass on) the local traditions and values. This will guarantee that Calabria's mountain villages will survive, although most may shrink in size. One cannot help but conclude this because the value systems rooted here are too strong, and the people's firm belief in family, faith and nature is central to their lives. Their traditions and values built over thousands of years, and the source of their strength, has fostered a resilience which is industructable.

CHAPTER VI:

The Making Of The Calabrian "Imprenditori"

(La Creazione Di Calabrese Imprenditori)

*"That a single mind could
anticipate the growth of knowledge.
The imagining of things that are to be."*

— The biographer Siren
commenting on Leonardo da Vinci

After driving my rental car for a month, it became very dirty with the night time dampness and the dusty roads due to the dry summer heat. It needed to be washed, but there are no car wash businesses in the mountain villages of Calabria. Then I thought that one of the young boys in Angoli might like the job to earn a little spending money, so I offered the job to 11-year-old Antonio Scalise and paid him 5 Euro in advance to demonstrate my sincerity. The opportunity pleased him; he took the money and we arranged for him to wash the car on the following day in the afternoon. About a half-hour later he approached me and returned the 5 Euro, saying he was busy tomorrow. Possibly he went home and told his mother, and she had him return the money being suspicious of the *"Americano."* I may never know, but I now believe I understand better why he did decline. I also asked some of the friends I am closest to here if they knew of someone who could wash and iron my shirts, but no one came forward with a candidate. The people here are fiercely independent, and they know how to take care of themselves and their own. Anything that might remotely suggest some form of servitude is immediately rejected given their centuries of intrusions and hardships.

My attempt to create a new Calabrian *"imprenditore"* failed, but I am puzzled why there are no children with lemonade stands or selling their own homemade cookies, or offering to wash home owners front steps. It could be that doing chores for others is expected if asked because everyone here is family or friend. Despite this personal mystery, I can assure you there is no lack of Calabrian *"imprenditori"* in Serrastretta, Angoli or any of the other villages. However, this area does have its examples of legitimate new business ventures that failed. For example, local personality Dalida opened two restaurants, now closed; one an outdoor nature amusement park. And the comune of Amato funded and operated a grand hotel, restaurant, banquet facility to attract tourism and provide jobs, but it now sits there empty on its hilltop as a stark reminder of a scheme too late for its time due to the growth of agritourism and the many *"agritourismo"* boutique properties that have opened. I drove up the long driveway to the Hotel Virginia, named for the woman who donated the property, and pulled up to the front door as if I were a guest checking in. You could tell it was once a beautiful setting, but today its boarded-up appearance reminds you of a haunted house in a horror movie. It would make a great filming location.

The Energetic, Talented Couple

In this chapter, I will describe the motivations of various *"imprenditorei"* from a wide variety of businesses: a restauranteur, a consultant (events promoter), a market/café owner, a logger, a mural artist, a furniture manufacturer, and others. Each one is very different, which you will see; but their commonalities drive them to succeed, and the role that resilience plays in this will be examined. One of the very first interviews I conducted for this chapter was with my cousin Sabrina Mazzei and her husband Massimo Iuliano (P38). They are my landlord and are fortunate enough to own five or six properties in Angoli. They are a unique couple, quite different from the average parents of young children. Both are well educated with separate professional careers, and even though they aspire to succeed, they are dedicated to Angoli and will not leave.

Sabrina and Massimo have two very well-mannered children, Jacopo age 10 and Gaia age eight. I see them daily playing with the other children and they are always very respectful to adults. Sabrina, age 39, is a special education school teacher with two university educations, one in languages (English and German) and the other in working with handicapped children. It is unusual to find a young couple in Angoli, each pursuing a career. Typically, a woman like Sabrina would be a "stay-at-home" wife and mother. To her, resilience is best defined by how you respond to the every-day challenges of life.

Massimo, age 44, is employed as a field services consultant by Simpool, a large logistics company, and he is often called upon to travel to Sicily, Naples, Rome and other Italian locations to help solve customer problems. He does not have university degrees, but he is both a civil engineer and a surveyor because of his technical school education. I have personally had a great deal of interaction with him in the design and construction of what I hope will be my permanent residence in Angoli, and I can say without reservation that he is an extremely talented individual. I nicknamed him Leonardo after my hero, and it is not an exaggeration. When it comes to design, construction, fabrication or repair, there are few more talented. The home he and his family live in, he completely redesigned and reconstructed from the inside out, doing much of the labor himself. He did the same for the apartment (or B&B) where I currently reside, and he is doing it again for the adjoining unit which I hope to soon occupy. On the first floor of B&B Two is a garage space which Massimo will turn into a local museum. The hallway leading from my new front door to the stairs up to the apartment will have a glass wall with a full view of the small museum.

There are many houses or properties in Angoli and the other mountain villages either unoccupied, abandoned, decaying or condemned. Virtually no resale market exists and the few being renovated simply provide better living conditions for current residents. It is understandable why there are individuals or families who own multiple properties; when an older generation passes, those remaining younger relatives are willed the property, and unless they use or maintain it, age, disrepair and decay set in. Owning multiple properties in no way makes you a Calabrian real estate *"imprenditore."* I was shown a house for sale with good interior space and a garden, but the family from a nearby village that owns it wants 45,000 Euro for it. Add to this figure another 30,000 to 40,000 Euro for renovation and it would be a very nice home few could afford; and it would never resell for the amount invested.

Massimo does not see himself as an *"imprenditore,"* and he says he has little interest in becoming one. However, I would bet he will because in pursuing what he likes to do best it may be a natural course, but it will not be in real estate. Creating and building things are his talent and his passion, and as he matures in this field, his skills will demand that he do related things on a larger scale. He expressed little interest in accumulating wealth, but he does have a plan for things he would like to do once he reaches retirement age. Both *"rappresentare"* outstanding citizenship as Massimo and Sabrina are an instrumental part of their community's long-term survival; and in doing so, they are a living example of resilience.

Breaking With Tradition to Succeed

Earlier in Chapter III, when describing Serrastretta, I referred to the Gallo Pastricciria as an outstanding pastry shop where I spend many hours meeting people and conducting interviews. It is, by far, the busiest establishment in town, but it was not always that way. The owners, Pier Luigi (Louie) Gallo, 65, and his wife Rita Mancuso, (P39) 57, started the business 40 years ago in pursuit of Louie's dream. He was well trained as a pastry chef in Rome but he was born in Serrastretta as were his parents and grandparents. and to both realize his dream and pursue his bride to be, he returned to Serrastretta to follow his dreams. They became true partners in marriage and in business, and now after building their highly successful enterprise, they have transferred ownership to their 31-year-old son Pier Pauolo. The Gallo's also have a 35-year-old daughter, Frederica, who is university educated in liberal arts and lives elsewhere.

Rita spoke very openly to me about their early struggles. Not only did they highly leverage the business by borrowing a substantial amount of money to purchase their main street location, fixtures and equipment, but they equally shared the ownership and the workload, he in the pastry kitchen and she out front serving customers. To them, this was the easier part of persevering and demonstrating resilience. The greater challenge was acceptance by their customer base. Here was a young local girl from one of Serrastretta's founding families, under 20 years of age, fulfilling what was considered a man's role 40 years ago. Most of the male customers considered it inappropriate for this young woman to be serving them; she should, instead, be serving only a husband.

Rita credits their success to their true partnership, their perseverance and their resilience. To them, quality of product is important; but even more so is their friendly attitude, always treating customers with kindness and respect. Louie agrees wholeheartedly. From my personal interaction with their son Paolo this business philosophy has been passed to the second generation. They are true Calabrian "*imprenditorei*."

Happy to be Working 365 Days a Year

In 1985, there were two small markets in Angoli; now there is only one. When one of the markets closed, it gave Carmelo Mazzei, 55, and is wife Rosetta Bruni, (P40) 50, the opportunity to open a new market in 1992. They were living in a small upstairs apartment in an old house, but they took a risk and leased space for a café/bar and market in a large house on the main street. Carmelo wanted to stay in Angoli, and he was willing to sacrifice in those early years to both learn the business, without previous experience, and run it single-handed while Rosetta was caring for their four-year-old son and a new baby daughter. Their son Paolo, now 28, is a career military officer, and their daughter Concetta, 24, is a police officer in Rome working at the penitentiary. Neither of the two children will return to Angoli to continue the business once Carmelo and Rosetta retire.

When the café and market became well established, they bought the house where they were living, Carmelo spending most of his time both refurbishing and adding on to the house while Rosetta worked at the business with the two small children at her side. The house sits on the edge of a cliff, and to reach it, you must descend an extremely steep driveway, so steep I was not sure I could make it all the way to the bottom without falling forward. The original house before refurbishment must have already been very old; the small barn where the sheep bedded down still stands. Both Carmelo and Rosetta climb the steep driveway at least twice every day. Even today, after making a success of their business, the couple works tirelessly. They have no employees other than themselves, and it requires 10-hour days; open for business 365 days a year, even on Christmas Day in the morning. The café/market is open from 7:00am to 7:00pm, and until 8:00pm in the summer, and closed daily for two hours at mid-day. Fortunately, Carmelo's father, Paolo, lives a few doors away, and he often closes.

The couple never take a day off or go somewhere for a vacation. I asked both if they ever get bored or frustrated with their constant routine. "No," they said, because of constantly being around customers and friends; and from my own observation, it readily shows. Rosetta has a very outgoing personality and a great sense of humor, always smiling and joking about something; and for the many hours I have spent with them, I have never seen them argue. If you want to know the latest gossip in Angoli, Rosetta is the one to talk to. Both look forward to retirement, Carmelo wanting to travel and Rosetta desires life in a big city. Every so often when I was at the market buying a few items, I noticed Rosetta would slip a small coin or two into her apron pocket, then I began dropping some small change in. She told me it was her "mad money" being saved for when she goes to Milan and Lake Como. Despite this difference in their retirement vision, I am positive they will find a way to accommodate both. In Calabria, you do not spend your life of resilience without bringing it to a successful conclusion. Their story will have a happy ending.

Home to Stay, and Loving It

One of the most fascinating and personable individuals in Angoli is Gaetano Lucia (nicknamed Gaetch) (P41), and although he is not technically an "*impenditore*," I would say he is a quasi-*impenditore.* Now 58 years old, as a young very handsome man he was filled with an adventurous spirit and spent much of his time travelling abroad touring foreign countries by motorcycle. He did marry at one point in his life, but he is now divorced and has a 20-year-old daughter living in London. Gaetch is today the manager of the restaurant/bar in Angoli, but if you were to walk in as a new customer, you would think he is the owner. He takes great pride in his work and loves his hometown village and its people. The restaurant/bar is owned by his cousin in Catanzaro and operates several other restaurants in the surrounding area.

The restaurant in Angoli has had a difficult past. Its location on the piazza of the San Giuseppe church is in the very center of town is ideal, however, making it a successful venture is difficult due to the limited population. It thrives in the summer when many relatives of residents come to visit for their holiday. In the winter, the restaurant struggles. Gaetch has made a success of the slower months with dedication and hard work. He had no previous food service experience, although he was a sales representative for a variety of products including food. Originally, the restaurant was first opened by local artist Dino Iuliano, but his efforts were not successful; then the building owner was going to give it a try, but he never opened despite making some cosmetic improvements. The business was then closed for several years before Getch and his cousin reopened.

Gaetch (P42) is very happy for the opportunity to work in Angoli, and now, at this stage of his life, he is content to live just one block away adjacent to his childhood home where his mother still resides. For him, life is a constant challenge of adapting to new situations, and that pleases him. Judging from some old photos of Gaetch he shared with me, you could tell he was a very trim, tall handsome young man; and now at his age, like most men, he struggles with the reality of not being as appealing to women as he was in his former years. Even for this, he calls upon his resilience.

A Man of Vision Personified

The best words to use when describing Antonio Molinaro (P43) 49, of Serrastretta are "a man of vision." He is truly an *"imprenditore"* (entrepeneur). Born and raised in Lamezia Terme, he is a graduate in finance/accounting of the University of Bologna, the oldest university in Europe. He calls himself a businessman/consultant whose job is helping others to realize their dreams. I questioned him on why he and his family live in Serrastretta, and he turned to point out his office window at the mountains and said there is no place this peaceful and beautiful. He and his wife Tiziana Maruca have two young daughters, Rebecca, 13, and Greta, eight. His wife is fluent in English and works at the Lamezia Terme airport.

When we discussed resilience, he emphasized his primary motivation using the words curiosity and challenge, and said he loves turning negative events into positives, thereby achieving both short-term and long-term success for his clients. He believes strongly in the viability and survival of Serrastretta and he is more than willing to take business risks to make that happen. His faith in Calabrians and the people of Serrastretta to him is not an over-exaggeration. In his words, they wear big shoes and have big minds from keen intuition; they create energy. One of Antonio's many visions is to one day be the sole sponsor of the Serrastretta Museum. Odds are, he will. There is no doubt, Antonio Molinaro is a remarkable Calabrian example of biographer Siren's words at the beginning of this chapter: "the imagining of things that are to be." For example, he is working with me on the rights to translate and publish this book for the Italian and EU markets.

Turning Gold and Gem Stones Into Life

Francesco Gallo (P44) established his jewelry business in Serrastretta 18 years ago after starting his career in the restaurant business. Because of an injury, he was unable to be on his feet for long periods of time and continue in the food industry. Therefore, he chose a new field, training in Naples and Cosensa to be a jeweler and goldsmith. His business, *LORY Preziosi (Gioielleria Laboratorio Orafo)* is thriving and he attracts customers from as far away as 75 kilometers. He possesses the skills of a true artisan as well as an *imprenditore*.

He explained his true motivation for his work was its creativity, and he has brought his laboratory up to state-of-the-art standards. He is the only craftsman for miles around using laser technology, an accomplishment he is most proud of. His assistant and associate, Giovanni Morrone works closely with Francesco in the creation of fine jewelry pieces, something I can personally attest to because he fabricated a beautiful ring for me.

The three of us talked about resilience, and they defined it as simply working and living from the heart. They said the people of Calabria have always worked with their hands for survival, and they too, do the same. Being from Calabria and Serrastretta carries with it a pride in its people, and provides a great source of wealth.

The Butcher, No Baker, No Candle Stick Maker

The meat *(carne)* most widely consumed by Calabrians is pork *(maiale),* and Adriano Mazza (P45) 52, sells the very best at his butcher shop *(macelleria)* in Serrastretta. He also sells poultry *(pollame),* rabbit *(coniglio),* and baby goat *(capra).* Just recently, he moved his shop onto the main street for greater customer exposure, and, he said, to reduce his cost. Veal *(vitello),* or beef, is also widely consumed, but it is far different from the US product. Technically, veal is from a calf that has only been fed on it's mother's milk, but in Italy, *vitello* refers to any young beef after it has switched to being grass fed; and it lacks the taste and marble texture of US western beef, although still very good.

Adriano was born and raised in San Pietro Apostolo, only a few kilometers from Serrastretta, and he has always been in the meat cutting business having received technical diplomas in his chosen field. The meat he sells is bought from a variety of private vendors because of its quality, and it is always a government inspected product.

He credits the fresh air of the mountains as the source of the people's strength and thinks resilience comes naturally to them. This, in combination with a strong family culture where parents instill the importance of traditions in their children, creates a strong community that is indestructible. "Our faith and the preservation of our natural environment are critical to a small community like Serrastretta," concluded Adriano.

From Horseshoes to Decorativbe Ironwork

It was not that many years ago, less than 100, when the streets in Angoli were much narrower and not wide enough to accommodate cars and trucks. Before engine powered vehicles arrived in the small mountain villages, the people used horse and mule drawn carts, and animals wore shoes, fitted and made by the local blacksmith. Fabio Lucia's grandfather and father were blacksmiths with their foundry on the first floor of their home about two blocks up the hill from the church, and now Fabio (P46) is the third generation to carry on the business; but he does not make horseshoes any longer. Instead, he is a highly skilled iron worker using the latest technology to create gates, fences, railings, table bases and a host of other metal decorative products for individual home owners, businesses and some government work. As the generations before him, his shop is on the first floor of his home, but it is located above the town center in Neuovo Angoli. He resides there with his wife and four-year-old son Giuseppe.

When I was touring his shop, he told me his passion is for forging iron and he loves the opportunity to create new things and find innovative ways to use his sophisticated equipment and his hands. His father taught him the basic skills, but he also trained under masters of the trade in both Sicily and northern Italy. Fabio has also studied electronics in technical school and periodically attends technical seminars to keep current with developments in his trade.

We talked at length about the people of Angoli and what it is that makes his village so special. He said, "We are deeply rooted in our traditions," and he described the Angolese characteristic for resilience as people's ability for "Solving problems and getting the job done." Fabio elaborated further by talking about the great suffering of the past and the present-day desire for redemption. In an environment which historically was based on agriculture and livestock production, if this is where you choose to remain, "You must now innovate and use your energies, pushing yourself to look forward and see things in a new way," Fabio concluded.

Ågritourism Takes Root

In Chapter II, I wrote about spending three days at the Agritourismo E Torre just outside of Serrastretta; and I have been back there a few times getting to know Marco Molinaro (P47), the owner and chef. He is assisted in the business by his parents and a brother, all of whom live in a small cluster of houses on property. There are only three well-appointed guest rooms that can house nine guests, and there are plans to add a few more, but Marco says the expansion is at least three or more months away. The restaurant is very spacious and can easily accommodate large family dinner parties and banquets. The family started the business in 2007, and Marco, at age 33, has had ample culinary training judging from the many plaques and certificates on the restaurant walls. Marco has a passion for cooking and the kitchen, mainly, he says, due to the local environment and its food traditions. "Nature and the soil are the ingredients for a long life," he believes. He went on to tell me that faith and family are the basics of life because combined they provide true value.

We, of course, talked about resilience and the future of the greater Serrastretta community. The key for the Molinaro family and E Torre is, in Marco's words, "To face life every day with a positive attitude." And he is not worried or afraid of the future, he has faith "…that God and our traditions will allow Serrastretta to survive."

Enough Chairs For Everyone

Being here in Serrastretta, "The City of the Chair," it seems appropriate to conclude this chapter with my interview with Pino Palletta (P48) a 50-year-old successful chair and table manufacturer located on the eastern edge of town. His factory is well equipped with up to date woodworking machinery, and he has a handsome showroom displaying the many different styles of chairs and tables he produces. Pino is the third generation to manage the business started by his grandfather in 1900. His mother, Giovanna, is a Scalise, thus indicating his family is well entrenched in the community. The company sells throughout all of Italy and does a limited amount of exporting, providing good jobs for his eight employees. Now, after 30 years in the business, Pino spends much of his time cultivating the market which consists primarily of restaurants and both private and public contract work.

To Pino, of course, the forest, as the source of his raw material "…is a precious asset and must be safeguarded." His chairs and tables are made of solid wood. No laminates or composite materials are used, and his first choice is always local raw materials although he does use some imported wood from Eastern Europe. The primary woods used are beech and chestnut oak.

"Here we are surrounded by chestnut woods that are the lungs of our land," he says. When talking with him it is very obvious he takes great pride, not only in his products, but from his local surroundings and its natural resources.

He is concerned, however, about the future of his community, not only because of the exodus of the young, but also because there are too few people learning the crafts that have sustained the people here for so long. Serrastretta still remains a special place, says Pino, thanks to the few who are trying to hang on to traditions and at the same time create positive, new things. He believes the people will never lose their resilience because "We have the ability to face all the difficulties daily life offers, in a positive way, without quitting so we can go forward day after day," he proclaimed.

Now that you have met some of the truly talented imprenditori of Serrastretta, you be the judge about how and why their values and their resilience will continue to move their community forward for many generations to come. They share much in common, and it is not to generate wealth, but rather to survive in a manner which they have come to cherish. Surprisingly, there were a few people who agreed to be interviewed, but when it came time to sit down with them, they always found a reason to cancel or delay; and I was never sure why. One individual stands out because he is a very prominent citizen of Angoli and an extremely successful businessman. He is Silvio Mancuso, the first cousin of the Silvio Mancuso discussed above. I am well acquainted with his office manager, Irene Mazzei, and I made at least six visits to his office without getting anywhere. My final pleading to him was a letter, in Italian, stating he needed to be in the book because of his prominence. The reason for his refusal will probably remain a mystery.

RESILIENCE

CHAPTER VII:

Points Of View From Down The Mountain, And Across The Strait

(Punti Di Vista Da Giu Dalla Montagna, E Attaverso Lo Stretto)

*"...the true joys of Calabria
are its simple pleasures."*
— Karen Haid
CALABRIA, The Other Italy

Out of necessity to take care of personal business matters, and for shopping, I was quite often in Lamezia Terme, a large, very busy place with crowded sidewalks, traffic jams and noise. Every time I start the drive back up the mountain, I wonder to myself just what the city people think of the mountain villages, and its people, less than an hour's drive away. I decided to find out.

Karen Haid, quoted above, described Calabria as follows: "It is a place where a slice of pecorino cheese or sausage can still be savored as people have done for centuries. The tastes are simple yet complex, to be enjoyed in company, seemingly simple, yet equally complex." This description fits all of Calabria, whether in the city or a mountain top village, but the similarities between city dwellers and mountain people seems to end there. One of the first city residents I spoke with was a remarkable woman named Daniela Bilardi (P49) who I had met several months ago because she is a friend of Sonia Bellezza. Daniela was born in Lamezia, but was educated at the University of Rome, after which she spent 25 years there. Now at age 56, she is back in Lamezia (Gizzerria, outside the city), raising her two adopted daughters, sisters from Armenia.

She loves living very close to the sea, and told me she could not live in the mountains, although she appreciates the villagers high above Lamezia are very fortunate because of their simple life style and their closeness with nature. They may have fewer possessions than city dwellers, she said, but they know happiness; and they epitomize the Calabrian character of resilience because they have the capacity to adapt, are warm and friendly, honor their family ties and cling to their traditions. Daniela concluded our conversation by telling me Calabrians are a special breed, mainly because of their multi-cultural beginnings.

On one of my trips to Lamezia, I made it a point to stop at my favorite *pasticceria* Caffetteria Falvo on Via Aldo Moro near where I first enter the city from the mountains above. I decided I would park myself there and engage in random conversations looking for people who could speak some English and would be willing to be interviewed. One young woman who worked behind the café bar spoke very good English, and I informed her what I was attempting to do. After about 45 minutes, she motioned to me and introduced me to Angelo Falvo, the owner's son, who spoke some English. He was with two of his friends, one of whom was very fluent in English, which led to the four of us sitting down at a table for an open discussion. I had already prepared some questions, and the three young men understood exactly what we were going to discuss.

Angelo's friends (P50) were Raffele Cortese, 31, and Luca Ferrise, 34, and they all seemed very pleased with the opportunity to participate. Raffele is a graduate of the University of Milan with a degree in English literature, so he led with responses and helped his friends with detailed explanations of my questions. We talked about Calabrian characteristics in general and the specific differences between the people in the mountain villages and the city residents of Lamezia. The word "passionate" quickly came to the surface, and how Calabrians "put passion into everything they do." Our work ethic is one of our most recognized characteristics, they told me, using the expression *"Lovorare come un mulo"* which obviously translates to "work like a mule." The interesting caveat in this Calabrian trait is the people enjoy working hard and it gives them pride to put food on the table for their family.

Raffele, Luca and Angelo summarized their opinions for me by saying how lucky they are to be Calabrians, not only because of the wonderful food, but also because of the vast variety of the natural environment that surrounds them every day. As they were leaving Falvo's (P51), all three smiled when one of them said, "We have the natural wonders of the mountains, the sea, the forest and historical landmarks all within minutes of one another."

On an early spring day when I was in Lamezia, I passed by a high-end bed store named Dorelanbed; and knowing I would be furnishing a new apartment in about six months, I stopped in to get some idea on pricing. The clerk was a middle-aged woman who was eager to show me her collection. After she gave me the tour and some prices, which seemed very high, I told her about this book and asked if she would be willing to answer a few questions about the character of Calabrians and about the people in the mountain villages. She agreed.

The clerk's name is Roberta Piro (P52), 48, who lives in Cosensa, a good hour's drive away. She and her family moved to Calabria from Puglia, the region just northeast of Calabria, when she was a baby. I found it surprising she has a degree in architecture from the University of Florence, but she uses her knowledge to help customers with room design and to explain the technical features of Dorelanbed's beds and their construction.

To Roberta, Calabrian people are very human because they are strong but extremely gentle, always ready to help others in difficulty. She knew little about the people high above her in the mountain villages, but knows their reputation is based on their strong family bonds and religious beliefs. She described herself as very religious and talked about how important the family is because to her "It is the family, most of all, that guides you through all the choices in life." We talked about the source of resilience, and there is no question in her mind that it is passed down through the family, both in raising children and through genetics.

The Journey Across the Strait

On my 227th day in Calabria, I crossed the Strait of Messina to spend two days in Sicily. My first impression of the city of Messina was of its architecture, as it appeared more classical than in Calabria. Messina has one of the famous duomos (P53) in all of Europe; its organ is said to be the second or third largest in Europe, and its clock tower movement every day at noon rivals that of Budapest. The tower is adorned with large golden figures that rotate and move in and out of the tower.

Immediately after arriving, I positioned myself in the lobby of the three-star Royal Palace Hotel for my first close observations of the people, thinking it would be a good place for random interviews. Again, I was incorrect with this assumption, so I set out on foot to see what else I could find. I was in Massina to gather opinions from Sicilians about Calabria and its people. One of the first things I did after setting out was to ask a well-dressed middle age woman the directions to the cathedral. She turned out to be most helpful and led me there on foot. Her English was minimal, but we chatted on the way giving me an opportunity for first impressions. This very brief interview with Cetty Barbera gave me my first clue that Sicilians see little difference in character; she told me the resilience factor is the same.

After she departed, I sat down at an outdoor café for a *caffee americano,* and I noticed two young men standing near my table engaged in serious conversation. Several beautiful young women came by and greeted them, but did not stay. I then interrupted their conversation, asked if they spoke English and would like a *caffee*. They answered both questions in the affirmative, and we then began a lengthy conversation. Both were University of Messina law students from Sicily. Their English was quite fluent, and when they learned about my research, they became very interested and talkative.

I had just met Victorio Silvestri and Alessandro Barbera (P54), age 20 and 19. Vitorio did most of the talking and impressed me with his knowledge of Italian history, his favorite subject. They have been to Calabria several times to ski, and the love the Calabrian food.

They believe the character of Sicilians and Calabrians is very similar, with the exception of Sicily being an island with its long history has made Sicilians more rebellious. Victorio made this observation: "If you are from Sicily, you must know and understand Calabria; and if you are from Calabria, you must know and understand Sicily." He spoke about the Greek influence on Sicily, and all of southern Italy, using the words *"Magna Graecia"* to describe it. He is a true history buff, a top scholarship student, and has twice gone to New York to participate in university student United Nations sessions. He also spoke proudly about his family, telling me in 1976, his grandmother was the second woman ever to be elected to the Italian Parliament.

I left these two young men totally impressed, knowing I had just met future Sicilian leaders.

By this time, it was just past midday, so I walked a bit more and found a small covered patio restaurant, *Past'ovo*, where I was served by a charming young woman who spoke excellent English and was familiar with Calabria. Angela DeLuca displayed a strong character, was self-taught in English, and was knowledgeable about Calabria. Her father was a sales agent for a Sicilian woman's clothing manufacturer and traveled often to Calabria. She would accompany him on his sales trips. She thinks Calabria is a very beautiful place, but too often forgotten.

Angela is a strong believer in the value system based on family, faith and nature, and thinks Sicilians have lost some of these qualities, while Calabrians have not. She made this simple comment to me: "You can choose to live happily or miserably." When she said this, I immediately thought of Angoli.

After a light lunch, I made my way back to the Royal Palace Hotel, where I parked myself there at the lobby bar. I noticed there were quite a few Italian national police officers staying there. I engaged one of them in conversation and learned he and his fellow officers were there training in immigration policy and administration. Vincenzo Sodano (P55) only had a few minutes to speak, and even though he is from Rome, he understands that the mountain people of Calabria live longer because of their natural environment, the food, the water and the air.

The following day, I decided to begin my journey back to Calabria a few hours earlier than planned, traveling by hydrofoil across the strait to Reggio Calabria, and then by train to Lamezia Terme. During the hour and a half train ride, I engaged a young man in conversation. He was 28-year-old Danieli Trunfio (P56) from Calabria who was fluent in English, having spent a year in Australia. He spoke very proudly about his Calabrian heritage and was very well versed in its culture and traditions.

He read with great interest the prospectus on this

book and was anxious to order a copy.

As I neared the completion of my Sicilian experience, I realized that the Sicilians I spoke with displayed greater than expected knowledge of Calabria. They seemed to know more about Calabria than Calabrians know about Sicily. And, what intrigued me the most is this: Sicilians and other Italians outside of Calabria seem to exhibit a greater respect for Calabria than Calabrians realize. They have been beaten down and trod upon for so long, that it is now time for them to rise up with pride and claim their true place in Italy.

CHAPTER VIII:

An Academic Perspective On Resilience

(Una Prospettiva Accademica Su Resilienza)

"And like Einstein, da Vinci had a problem with authority. He often seemed defensive about being an 'unlettered man,' as he dubbed himself with some irony, but had little patience with the 'foolish folk' who thought less of him. 'They strut about puffed up and pompous, decked out and adorned not with their own labors, but by those of others,' he wrote in one of his notebooks. He was by his own words, a disciple of experience and experiment – 'Leonardo da Vinci, discepollo della sperientia,' he once signed himself. That approach to problem-solving was nothing short of revolutionary, foreshadowing the scientific method developed more than a century later by Francis Bacon and Galileo Galilei. And it elevated da Vinci beyond even the smartest of his peers. "Talent hits a target that no one else can hit," wrote the German philosopher Arthur Schopenhauer. 'Genius hits a target no one else can see.' "

— By Walter Isaacson
Time Magazine , Vol. 190 No. 22-23, 2017

A cademics, men of letters, the world over have been studying the evolution of human civilizations for a very long time; certainly, they must have theories or opinions about the role of resilience on man's character. I decided to investigate and delve into this issue right in the "back yard" of the Calabrian people. Calabria has a host of very good universities specializing in the humanities, sciences, medicine, engineering and architecture; and there are any number of independent researchers on the history and culture of southern Italy.

The Dean of Local Knowledge

One of the most highly respected academics in the greater Serrastretta area, and in all of Calabria, is Professor Mario Gallo (P57). He has authored several books on the area's history and its people; and is considered one of the leading experts on the immigration of the people of Serrastretta to the United States, Canada, Australia and South America. His book, *Serrastretta, Fonti Di Una Communita Operosa*, is considered very authoritative. It even features one of the bronze carved panels from the main doors of the church in Serrastretta. Professor Gallo's home is in one of the oldest sections of Decollatura, and from the outside, the connected houses on the narrow street have a very ancient and worn look. He greeted me at his front door, and when you enter, you are immediately impressed with its very tasteful up to date décor. It is refined and conservative, and the professor's in-home two room office is filled with wall lined book shelves. The atmosphere spoke of knowledge, as did the professor himself who was very neatly attired. You could visualize him walking into a classroom, books in hand.

He is now retired after 44 years of teaching the humanities: Italian, history, geography and Latin. He is a graduate of the University of Messina in Sicily. During his last years in the field of education, he served as director or superintendent of the high school system in Calabria.

Professor Gallo and I spent an hour and a half together discussing the character of the local people and their resilience. The key word he kept coming back to in our conversation was "independent," and he elaborated with a number of examples. He told me the people of Serrastretta have always exercised their independence, it is "in their blood," and they have always demonstrated a complete sense of community because of their ability to cooperate with one another. His research has proven to him how unique this characteristic is, even throughout Calabria. Some of the examples he shared with me included the church in Serrastretta from its very beginning. It was founded in 1398 as an independent church, meaning it was not affiliated with any other parish and could fully operate on its own; because that is what the people wanted.

The governance of Serrastretta is yet another example. Serrastretta is a comune, meaning it is run by a council of representatives from its incorporated villages, and operates more as a cooperative. This, in and of itself, is unique because it was 300 years ahead of its time in Calabria.

Serrastretta has always prided itself on being a place of specialization where the people cooperate to reach a perfection in their skills and trades. An example is the manufacture of reed seat chairs and other furnishings. The professor told me the story of how Serrastretta was the first in all of Calabria to establish an electric utility cooperative, and brought power to the village 40 years ahead of Catanzaro, the capital city of Calabria.

He showed me some of the other books he has published, including those containing the immigration records. Between 1901 and 1910, he said, 2,500 people from Serrastretta went to America. Those numbers included my grandfather in 1902 and my grandmother in 1903. When we concluded our visit, we shared a coffee and he suggested I should interview Angelo Aiello, secretary/director of the Dalida Association in Serrastretta because of his vast knowledge of local history.

Every Child is Taught With Love

During my first three month stay in Calabria, I met a teacher who also lives in Decollatura, but this academic teaches in Angoli where he specializes in helping children with severe mental handicaps. He is Luigi Anania (P58), 42, and single living with his parents. He has his university degree from the University of Bologna in history and philosophy, and unlike Professor Gallo, Luigi is fluent in English. He spent a number of his early professional years substitute teaching before he went back to school to earn his degree in special education, and he has been teaching in Angoli for the last six years.

Luigi told me the story of his grandfather immigrating to Australia where he worked on tobacco farms. Having visited his grandfather in Australia, Luigi was surprised to learn that his far away relative chose his location and his work very carefully to be as similar to his life in Calabria as possible. He found a small town with matching landscape and worked in tobacco farming to be close to the soil, because in Decollatura potato farming is a significant agricultural activity. Luigi related this story to demonstrate how important traditions are to Calabrians, like the slaughter of a pig which he participated in as a boy; even, Luigi said, the preservation of the Calabrian dialect (which uses Spanish, French and Arabic words) is important because it connects you to your identity, just like the local food and music.

We talked about resilience, and Luigi expressed how important this characteristic is to his work with disabled children; he thinks of himself as a psychologist and a teacher, telling me how important it is for the children's parents to show great resilience living with a bad situation. The parents must have the capacity to "bend." It is in their power to do so, and they must work with him to communicate "emotional knowledge" to their child, even when the child cannot speak.

Luigi also talked about nature as one of the keys to Calabrian character. He fully agrees that nature, along with family and faith, are critical ingredients fo resilience. To prove this, he told me an historical story going back to the early Roman Empire. There was a politician and philosopher named Catone serving in the Roman senate. He was an eloquent speaker, and when he was addressing someone in the senate, he would look at their hands and not their face. The reason: if the person's hands were not stained without dirt under the fingernails, he was not trustworthy because he had no direct connection to nature and to the soil.

A Language Teacher of Few, Well Chosen Words

In Angoli there is a retired teacher, Gaetano Mazzei (P59), who is also the father of Maria Cristina Mazzei, the woman living in the Venice area I wrote about in Chapter III. Gaetano, now 71, was a teacher of languages, Italian and French; and today he is very active in the Angoli community, even in the church. We only had the opportunity for a brief conversation, partly due to his lack of English. He credits Calabrian resilience to the willingness of the people to work hard and sacrifice, and they maintain traditions, even their religion, which will carry the Catholic Church *("Chiese Cattolica")* forward. The harmony of the people and their lack of anxiety will assure the survival of Serrastretta and its villages, Gaetano told me.

The Cardiologist With A Big Heart

I was told by some friends in Serrastretta that the most highly regarded doctor in town is Gaspare Mancuso (P60), a 61-year-old cardiologist, who just happens to be the first cousin of the Gaspare Mancuso, discussed in Chapter III, who lives in Fort Worth, Texas. Rita Gallo introduced me to Dr. Mancuso and we arranged to meet for an interview. We sat in the Gallo Café for more than an hour reviewing the opinions I was hoping to get from him. He took my written questions and said he would have his written response back to me in a week. As typical, it took him two weeks to respond, but his document was very well constructed and legible.

He has his medical degrees in internal medicine, cardiology and surgery, and you would expect that a man this highly educated would be living a more luxurious life in a major Italian city. He told me that "Certainly, every now and then, I am tempted to say 'Let's go live in the city,' but I go back to my fundamental belief that social relations in a small place are more humanistic, and, therefore, more rewarding." He very openly spoke about his love for his birthplace, his roots and his origin; and that his passion is to use his professionalism and his social and cultural commitment for the greater value of Serrastretta.

I was intrigued when he called upon an ancient Italian saying which paraphrased says "Big shoes strangle the mind, while work shoes open up the mind." In telling me this, he was philosophically giving me his description of the mountain people of Serrastretta and its villages. Dr. Mancuso went on to elaborate by saying the people's strength of "soul and action" is derived from the fact they have always had to defend themselves and fight against the "logic" of the "arrogant and wealthy." Like many others interviewed, Dr. Mancuso well understands the role that centuries of hardships have played in building the character of Calabrians. It was easy to discern his pride, not in being an accomplished doctor, but in being Calabrese, because he believes "We, the people of Calabria can adapt and survive in their own land because we grew up in simplicity...knowing how to give greater value to sentiments and affection, honest and constant work, rather than to material things," he concluded.

A Professor Who Remains Positive

Professor Enrico Mascaro (P61) is one who remains positive about everything Calabrian and about himself. At age 77, he lives with a terminal illness, saying in my interview with him, "No problem."

A life long teacher, and an expert in Calabria's demographics, he grew up in Tiriolo before beginning his career. His Jewish family originated in Spain and escaped persecution to Calabria hundreds of years ago. Professor Mascaro attended the University of Torino, and his advanced degrees are from the University of Messina where he studied modern Italian history.

Most of his teaching career was in Lamezia Terme, where over 30 years he was a superintendent in the school system. He was the first to start an English language program for elementary students as young as three years-of-age. Today, he lives in Serrastretta and is married to Rabbi Barbara Aiello. The couple work hand-in-hand on research projects uncovering the Jewish history of Calabrians. Enrico and Barbara's grandmothers were sisters.

The professor told me the story of a village near Angoli that originally had a synagogue, later turned into a Catholic church, and a Jewish quarter, remnants of which exist today. The village's name is Zangraona, and it is often visited and toured by visiting Jews who come to Serrastretta and Rabbi Barbara's synagogue.

We spent almost an hour discussing the characteristics of the Calabrian people. Professor Mascaro related stories of constant invasions and outside rule to demonstrate the toughness of the Calabrese, all the way back to Roman rule when people like Spartacus lead uprisings of slaves. Rome, he said, was never in favor of giving up slavery. "We, as Calabrians, are born to deal with problems and resolve them. Life is a challenge, and we are taught as children how to make the best of a bad situation," he told me.

I came away from our time together confident that the professor will, as he said, "...turn a negative into a positive." He will spend the rest of his days devoted to preserving the history of all Calabrians, regardless of their religious choice.

The learned men of letters you just met have a thorough knowledge and understanding of Calabria and its people, far beyond just being one of them. They have studied it, taught it and written about it; and their influence and that of other academics will help Calabrian culture and tradition, not only survive, but become more widely recognized.

CHAPTER IX

How Clerics Perceive Resilience

(Come I Chierici Si Percepiscono Resilienza)

"I want my church to shine. But I understand that everything, from our institutions to our innermost beings, are seen through a glass darkly. Arms outstretched, listening for the Word, and its echoing liturgy, I make my way forward, in bright hope."

— Elizabeth Scalia, an American Author, Blogger
"Why I Remain Catholic"

After spending three months in Calabria, I returned home to southern California for a break and to reconnect with my family. On my first Sunday at home, I went to mass at my home parish St. Thomas More Catholic Church in Oceanside, California to again observe and experience the stark differences between mass in Calabria and mass in the United States. This lead me to wonder if there were significant differences between clerical views on the importance of family, faith and nature (resilience) in the United States and southern Italy. Therefore, I sat down for a discussion and interview session with Reverend Michael Ratajczak, pastor at St. Thomas More; and even though this book is about the people of Serrastretta in Calabria, somehow leading off this chapter with Father Mike's views, does not seem inappropriate.

The Evolving Catholic Church In America

The quotation above by Elizabeth Scalia, an Italian American, was used by Father Mike in an article he wrote discussing the challenges faced by the Catholic Church in dealing with its weaknesses and exposed scandals. He called upon Elizabeth Scalia's words "I make my way forward, in bright hope," a statement very similar to the views of Calabrians when commenting on resilience. Ms. Scalia has authored several self-help books on faith and she is a well-known blogger on Catholic issues.

Father Mike is a priest who is not afraid to express his views on faith and current Catholic issues, and his positions are very liberal, somewhat unusual for a man of 70 years-of-age nearing retirement. He is truly a man of the people; in his parish, everyone is welcome regardless of religion, beliefs or life style. A parish visitor once said to him, "There is no judgement here!" To compare him to the priests who serve the parishes in Italy, one can only say they are at the extreme opposite ends of the spectrum. To Father Mike, religion, Catholic or otherwise, comes down to two things: love of God and love of neighbor. We talked at great length about how the institution of the Catholic Church has fallen far behind its lay members, especially in Italy and other European countries. This is true even in America he says, but not to as great an extent. Although Father Mike is not an

Italian descendant (but Polish), his brother is married to an Italian from a large family, many of whom are recent immigrants to the United States, and they live nearby in California. He understands and appreciates their positions on faith and the Church; and he was intrigued listening to my descriptions of Serrastretta and Angoli, the character, warmth and friendliness of the people there, and the value they place on family and community.

I asked Father Mike why Pope Francis has not done more in the face of the Church's decline and the scandals that plague it. His response was two-fold: first, the Church (the Vatican) is a highly political organization with many internal controlling forces in play, and second, Pope Francis has taken many actions to get issues on the table for discussion. He firmly believes issues like allowing priests to marry, more women involved in Church leadership roles even as priests, greater tolerance for gays and divorce will all come about. St. Thomas More now has a gay ministry within its community. Will the Church survive? Father Mike gave both a "yes" and a "no" answer. "Yes," he said, the Catholic faith will survive; but "no," he thinks the institution of the Catholic Church may eventually pass away, or in the least, drastically change. Today's more modern Catholics are more highly educated than in the past, they are individual thinkers who want to be part of a more tolerant community, one which they have some control over.

"Though divinely inspired, the Church is imperfect, because it is composed of imperfect human beings. We are a combination of virtue and vice, always in need of reform. We can be resilient if we keep our faith focused on Jesus and the Sacraments, not on people and structures in the institution," concluded Father Mike. He is convinced the Church will move forward beyond its old ways and its current scandals will not be easy and will take a long time. The Church suffers from a severe case of "clericalism," creating an atmosphere wherein Church leaders only listen to one another. Survival will require perseverance, adaptability and resilience on the part of many people. "I believe," said Father Mike, "It's not too late.

Some Skepticism, But Faith Prevails

Don Antonio Costantino has been the pastor of Beata Maria Vergine del Soccorso in Serrastretta for the last five years, replacing Don Luigi Iiliano who was transferred to a parish in Lamezia Terme. This change after Don Gigi was pastor in Serrastretta for only four years puzzles me. Why switch since Don Gigi was born and raised in Serrastretta and is so very popular among the people? After getting to know Don Antonio, I would describe him, at age 43, as a liberal compared to Don Gigi.

When I asked him why men generally avoid attending mass, he reminded me that at one time in the Church's history, only men attended. He views the future of the Church with some amount of skepticism, but he says he prays the rosary that it will self-correct. The Church today faces challenges from peoples' pursuit of education, care for the family and the many attractions the world now offers. But the strength of the people in Serrastretta and its villages comes from "their hard work, their faith and their traditions," he said. But he cautioned, "The Vatican is seen as far too rich, but we must have faith in the pope, and in the clergy, but not all of them."

When we talked about resilience, Don Antonio used the word "adaptation," stemming from a deep trust in yourself, with help and support from family and friends.

Don Antonio asked me to see him in Serrastretta after mass on a particular Sunday so we could complete the interview. During mass as I was sitting near the back of the church, I noticed Rabbi Barbara Aiello sitting in the front row. During the service, she did one of the readings, and when mass was over, she was invited to the pulpit. I was rather curious as to what would transpire. She told the sad story of Eduardo, a Jewish baby in Poland who was on a "cattle car" train to Auschwitz with his parents and how his life was spared with the help of a Polish Catholic family. To save his life, Eduardo's mother stuffed him inside a mattress and threw him off the train somewhere along the way. He was abandoned there in the snow when his cries were heard by a nearby family; he was rescued by them, given the name Eduardo and raised as one of their own. After the war and when he was grown, he was told of his past, what little is known of it. Rabbi Barbara quoted him as saying, "They gave me a name, Eduardo, and after the war told me I was Jewish. I am grateful to my mother who had the courage to throw me from the train and save me from certain death in Auschwitz. And I thank the Polish Catholic family who found me, named me and saved my life."

Two Sides of the Same Coin

The church of San Giuseppe in Angoli is beautiful on the inside due to its recent renovation, but it is worn and in dire need of fresh patching and paint on the outside.

This is due, I was told, to a shortage of funds; and unlike the church in Serrastretta, it does not have a full-time pastor. It does have two part-time pastors from nearby who share the duties, and I have gotten to know both quite well. Both are of African heritage and are fluent in Italian and English. Don Isaac is from the West African country of Togo, while Don Emmanuel was born and raised in London. Both are about the same age in their mid-forties.

The Roman Catholic religion has been practiced in Togo since the 1880's when it first became a German colony. Don Isaac grew up Roman Catholic and was educated for the priesthood in Switzerland and Italy. He displays a great sense of humor, judging from his homilies, which according to him is a family trait handed down from his father. I assumed he would be very talkative during our discussion, but I was surprised to discover he is a man of few words.

Mass is said at the Angoli church on Wednesday and Friday evenings and on Sunday morning by either one or the other priests. I sat down with Don Isaac after mass one Friday evening in the office behind the alter to discuss his views on his congregation and the Catholic Church in general. Don Emmanuel also happened to be present, and he participated in the discussion. Don Isaac comes from a multi-generational Roman Catholic family, and his full name is Isaac Marie Assogbavi. Both priests have an undying trust in the future of the Catholic Church, whether that be in Italy or elsewhere. When I asked Don Isaac if he thought of himself as a conservative or a liberal, my question came across as if absurd. His response was simply, "I am a Catholic." To both priests, that emphatically means you cannot love the Catholic Church without loving the whole Church. They make no distinction between the Roman Catholic faith and the institution (Vatican). "They are two sides of the same coin," they told me. Their faith in the future of the Catholic Church is absolute.

When we talked about the Calabrian character of the Angolese people, they fully recognize the strength that exists, and they credit it to two things: the local environment and heredity. They believe the resilience is genetic and the people of Calabria, Serrastretta, and Angoli are born with it.

A Priest Who Learns From the People

I finally met a cleric here who seems to be totally open-minded about the Catholic Church and its future. The attitude he displays could be the result of his youthfulness at age 42, but I believe it stems more from his relationship with the faithful. He hesitates calling himself a liberal, but he holds on to the firm belief his role is to learn from his congregation, and not the other way around. Most assuredly, he represents a breath of fresh air. He is Don Giovanni Morotta, pastor of Tiriolo's Church of Santa Maria della Grazie. We first met during my second visit to Tiriolo, the hometown of the Vincenzo Bevivino descendants, and I immediately knew he had much to offer for this chapter of the book. During his interview, he spoke much more openly than the other clerics I questioned; and his responses came across with an air of humility and honesty.

Don Giovanni told me he does not consider himself liberal or conservative, and said "I try to grasp what the

Spirit suggests to me as good, pulling out 'old things and new things' according to the situation I am in. He comes from a modest family in the town of Conflenti on the slopes of Mount Reventino near Catanzaro, and has been a priest for 12 years, the last nine in Tiriolo.

"Sometimes I get caught up in a human logic that discourages me, especially when faced with situations of scandals that are called to face the Church, but repeating to myself the words of the Master 'the gates of hell will not prevail,' I immediately turn back to hope and smile returns. I am sure of it, as the Pope recently said, 'the devil has the hours counted,'" he told me. Then he went on to express his views on the role of women in the Church. He referred to Mary as a model, and praised the "courageous, humble and hidden work of women." Making reference to the diversity of roles within the "Church family," Don Giovanni summarized his view on the female role with these words, "Our society offers us a self-referential idea that favors the individual, and this also insinuates itself within the Church which is made up of men, but it is much more evangelical to walk together, where one needs the other, the man and the woman."

Beyond his clerical role, Don Giovanni loves being a Calabrese and praised the area's natural wonders: the sea, the mountains, the forest, the water, even "the chili pepper, the onion, the olive tree..." He credits the Calabrese resilience to history and to the peoples' stubbornness to face life as it comes; and he called upon St. Paul's admonition about transforming every suffering into grace. "'When I am weak, I am strong.'"

Here is how Don Giovanni, in his concluding remarks to me, expressed himself about learning from the people:

"I have so much to learn from the faith of the people, it was often they who preceded me on the believing path. Those who suffer, those who entrust themselves and are capable of loving, despite everything, are ahead. This makes you understand the beauty of peoples' hearts and makes you bless God for the great gift of having received a community to love and grow together." The Catholic Church, in Italy and everywhere, needs more clerics like Don Giovanni Marotta.

The Good Sister With The Smile

There are two nuns who regularly assist the priests who serve the churches in Angoli, Migliuso and Cancello. One is Sister Micheline (P66) who always has a smile on her face and has always gone out of her way to speak to me. Her full name is Ngonge Limolo Michiline, a 36-year-old university educated black woman from the Republic of Congo who speaks English, French, Italian and her native language.

Sister Micheline was raised a Catholic by her parents and she takes the traditional conservative view of the other clerics from Africa, believing that women should not become priests. She told me she came to Italy to better experience the holy life of becoming a nun. She understands the subject of this book, that it is based on research of the peoples' origins in Serrastretta and its villages, but worries because she is new here, she does not yet fully understand them. The people here, she says, know the Christian life very well; and she referenced the many saints from southern Italy. But, she reminded me, there are also those who follow the devil and his "black magic," naming the Mafia.

She thinks the Calabrian people are wonderful because they organize their lives well to raise a family, building their homes and preparing their children for the future. They make the absolute best out of very little, the good sister concluded.

The clergy here in Italy seem to function with almost a blind faith, a faith based on an unquestionable loyalty to the Vatican. While their loyalty is admirable, their flocks, in general, take an opposite point of view. The widespread mistrust for Italy's governing bodies (the government, the Vatican and the Mafia) reinforces the clergy's blindness. Think about this: how could a priest in Italy reach the conclusion that he, himself, is not trusted? This is a difficult thing for anyone to accept, clergy or not.

CHAPTER X

The Bond Between Nature And Resilience

(Il Legame Tra Natura E Resilienza)

"On occasions of drought or flood there is not a word of complaint. I have known these field-faring men and women for thirty years, and have yet to hear a single one of them grumble at the weather. It is not indifference; it is true philosophy – acquiescence in the inevitable....They have the same forgiveness for the shortcomings of nature as for a wayward child. And no wonder they are distrustful. Ages of oppression and misrule have passed over their heads; sun and rain with all their caprice, have been kinder friends to them than their earthly masters..."

OLD CALABRIA
By Norman Douglas

The youngest child of my grandparents Rosario and Rosa Scalise Bevevino was Lorraine Bevevino Bengston who often commented how her parents would tell stories of how hard they worked in the gardens while growing up in Angoli. The love for the soil and nature's bounty continued uninterrupted throughout their entire lives.

Why, we might wonder, do the people of Serrastretta and its villages still continue to grow their gardens, raise chickens, pigs, goats and sheep when the foods they produce can be easily purchased at near-by markets? And why did Andrea Caruso in Chapter V explain to me how Calabrians understand and appreciate that apples come from a tree and not from the supermarket? And why do the ladies of Angoli spend hours and hours making gallons of their own *"pomodoro salsa"* for the winter months when a wide variety of commercial brands is widely available and inexpensive? And, finally, why did an Italian American restaurant owner from Pennsylvania, when describing with pride the influence of great Italians on the USA use these words: "My roots are deep in ancient soil, drenched by the Mediterranean sun and watered by pure streams from snow-capped mountains. My hands are those of the mason, the artist, the man of soil."

This love for the soil and nature's bounty can be traced back thousands of years to a time when Sicily became a distant garden for growing wheat and other crops to be shipped back to Greece. The Greeks and other Mediterranean peoples who populated Sicily used virtually all the level farmable land between the foot of the mountains and the shore line, particularly in the north and northwest of the island. Those peoples, the ancestors of today's Sicilians and Calabrians, have roots "...deep in ancient soil," and they survived for thousands of years honing their agricultural skills. They became masters of perseverance, adaptability and survival, using their resilience during times when nature seemed to work against them and foreign rule seemed to have no end. This mastery is in their blood; it is part of who they are.

In the Introduction for this book, it was mentioned that Leonardo da Vinci relied on nature as his teacher because he begrudgingly was not schooled in the Greek and Roman classics as "educated" young men should be. He bragged he was not a "man of letters." Biographer Martin Kemp in his book *LEONARDO,* wrote: "Although Leonardo claimed, with inverted pride, to be a man 'without learning' who relied only on 'experience,' he well knew that a great deal of important wisdom was locked in Latin treatises, and he went to considerable trouble to consult a wide range of authors on 'natural things,' both classical and medieval." For as genius as he was, Leonardo struggled with translating Latin texts.

But to Leonardo's credit, he did not miss the remarkable connection between the texts he did read in Latin and his own theories on nature and its direct connection to humans. According to Kemp, "The basic concept was that the body of the human being was a microcosm, mirroring in its whole and parts the microcosm, or greater world. It was not so much that the lesser and greater worlds literally looked similar, but that the principle of organization – of the fittingness of form to function in the context of universal flux – were shared at the profoundest level. Rules remain valid independently of the scale of the phenomenon." Kemp further suggests that the theories of classical Roman author and orator Seneca, who Leonardo presumably read, are rather consistent with the writings of the Renaissance genius in the early 16th century when he was dissecting cadavers and drawing internal human parts.

Seneca wrote: "The idea appeals to me that the earth is governed by nature and is much like the system of our own bodies in which there are veins (vessels for blood) and arteries (vessels for air). In the earth there are some routes through which water runs, some through which air passes. And nature fashions these routes so like the human body that our ancestors even called them 'veins' of water...as in our bodies, when a vein is cut, blood continues to ooze forth...so in the earth when veins are loosed or broken a stream or river gushes out."

A Man Committed to Preserving the Traditions of Harvest

It was around mid-day and I had walked to the bottom of *Via Crichi Sottano* when Roberto Talarico approached me and wanted to show me his gardens. We walked a few yards up the hill and he pointed out on the right a gently sloping garden full of very healthy-looking tomato, zucchini and bean plants. It was obvious he was very proud of his work. A little further up the road on the left, we stopped at a shed, and he backed out of it a large wheel barrow loaded with over-grown zucchini. We climbed further up the hill to some other sheds on the left, and I could tell by the foul odor there was livestock there. As we walked along side the sheds, Roberto opened some doors to reveal four large hogs. He proceeded to toss some zucchini to the hogs which they devoured.

After we went back down the hill, Roberto went into the cellar of his house and quickly reappeared with a bottle of his wine in hand, which he gave to me, again with great pride. I enjoyed the wine over the next several days.

During the days surrounding the first of a new year, it is traditional in the mountain villages to butcher a pig *("maiale")*. The process is tedious and takes hours of work by five or six hands, usually a family group that will share the spoils. Nothing is wasted, and the only parts of the animal not used are the eyeballs and the toe nails. Even the blood is rendered to make an edible substance like Nutella.

I was invited by Roberto (P67) to be at his hog shed at 7:30am, but the work started earlier, i.e. the building of a fire to boil water in a metal drum used to soften the animal's hair and continually rinse the skin. After the pig is killed by stabbing it in the neck, two men shave off all the hair using razor sharp large knives while two others constantly pour on the boiling water just ahead of the knives. Then it is scrubbed clean with a solution of salt and critus juice. It is white, smooth and clean as a baby's bottom. The work party consisted of Roberto, his young son, his wife, his father-in-law and three other men. All of the work takes place in an open shed while the kill is laying on a slatted table before it is hung by its hind feet and winched to the shed roof so its head is off the ground. The pig weighed between 180 and 200 pounds. The dissecting begins by removing the pork belly, but it is not until after the pig is completely cut apart that all the butchered pieces are weighed on an electronic scale.

During our conversations, I posed a series of questions to Roberto; one was why he and his family continue to slaughter pigs. He responded quite emphatically,

"I grow them and breed them for the genuine meat, not that of the markets, full of chemicals, and to keep the tradition alive. Like the vegetables and other foods I cultivate, they are deprived of chemical agents. I fertilize only with manure. We are without stress, and consume what I harvest without incident. My father left me this desire and tradition."

We talked about the soil and nature, and he told me most everything he and his family have comes from nature, their daily lives, the houses they live in, and they work to keep their surroundings "flowery and green." "If we lose this splendor," he said, "it would be a very serious consequence." Roberto loves Angoli and knows he will stay forever. "My life beat is here," he confided, "and with a little imagination and commitment, there is no more magical place." Roberto summarized his view of resilience with the word "love," love of the people and love of the soil.

Gardening Brings Her Closer to Nature

Based on the questions posed above at the beginning of this chapter, I sat down for an interview with Sabrina Mazzei's mother, Caterina Fiorentino (P68). In addition to Sabrina, she has two other daughters, Antonietta in Angoli and Mariagrazia in Rome. When I questioned her about her love of gardening, her immediate response was she has been doing it from the time she was a young girl; and in gardening, she is brought closer to nature with the guarantee that what she consumes is genuine and natural (organic).

"My food goes directly from the soil to my mouth," she said. In the past, she told me, times were hard, and there was suffering and little food, and it was difficult to survive. "You learned how to get by with just a few things." She went on to explain that in the past, everything Calabrians had came from nature: stone for buildings, wood for furniture, reeds for baskets and chair seats, wild plants such as linseed for fabrics, and other forest vegetation *("capana Italiano"),* and terracotta for containers. Plastic or other synthetic materials were nonexistent.

When we discussed resilience and its source in the Calabrian people, she responded by saying it is born out of suffering and hardship.

I asked Caterina about the decline in population and the young people leaving. Angoli will survive, she told me, because its valuable source of energy and well-being will not be lost. She gave me the example of her grandson who started a business in Cancello making and repairing wooden pallets. She happily concluded our conversation by telling me the more worldly possessions you have do not make you any happier. Then she proudly showed me photos of her mother and grandmother weaving fabric on a loom. She is truly a sage senior citizen of Angoli and has done a remarkable job of raising her three beautiful daughters in this remote, tiny village.

Calabrian Nouveau Cuisine – Bringing the Old Back to the New

Reportedly from many local sources, the best restaurant in Serrastretta is *Il Vecchio Costagna* which translates to The Old Chestnut. It is owned and operated by a highly accomplished chef, Delfino di Maruca (P69). Delfino learned his culinary skills in the north of Italy by working in a variety of restaurants, mainly in the region of Valle d'Aosta. His 30-year-old son Mattia is very active in the business with him and hopes to carry it on after his father retires. Delfino has been in the culinary profession for 36 years, and his Serrastretta restaurant is now in its 12th year.

The restaurant is, of course, very well appointed, but what you first notice upon entering is the establishment's devotion to chestnuts and mushrooms; and for very good reason. My interview was actually with both father and son, and the pride Mattia showed in his father's accomplishments was exuberant. They explained that in the 1970's and 80's, Calabrians began to recognize their own regional cuisine as something special that could rival dishes from the north. Their food was not to be looked down upon, and with that realization, Delfino began to use some of the long-forgotten ingredients for creating or recreating new dishes. The use of chestnuts, mushrooms and forgotten herbs were the key. The restaurant went back to making flour from chestnuts, and then used it to make forgotten pasta incorporating ricotta cheese and walnuts. Some of the other ingredients brought back to life were juniper berries and nettles from a wild forest plant.

In addition to the pasta, one of Delfino's signature dishes is a pork fillet with a juniper berry and chestnut cream sauce. These dishes have won national Italian culinary competitions, and Delfino and Mattia were proud to show me the award certificates. They also make wonderful deserts from chestnuts and figs, as well as a distinctive chestnut liquer.

When we discussed resilience, Mattia said that

suffering, anger and compassion for one another have shaped Calabrians, and they will do anything to keep their traditions alive.

Respect for the Area's Greatest Resource

There is no question that the forests on the mountains surrounding Serrastretta and its villages are the area's greatest natural resource. The forest provides a bountiful harvest of timber, game, mushrooms, chestnuts, herbs, clean water and air and an unequaled beautiful environment. "Not only does it provide all this," says Silvio Mascaro (P70), "it also provides a livelihood for many people and tax revenue for the government." Silvio, a commercial logger, explained to me how the people and the government go to almost extreme measures to preserve it.

"*Indusrria Boschiva, Commercio Lennami, Produzione Lego Da Ardere*" (Wood Industry, Timber Trade, Production Of Firewood) is how Silvio describes his business. He has five employees and operates five giant tractors and three trucks, and you are likely to see his employees and vehicles on the roadways several times a day. His customers include sawmills producing timber and packaging, power plants fueled by wood and firewood consumers for heating.

Silvio's two sons work in the business and will one day manage it. They are currently building their own homes on the site of the company's staging yard and equipment storage facility in *nuovo Angoli*. It is a large garage, on top of which the sons are building a two-story duplex home. From there, the panoramic view is spectacular, with a view of the seas both east and west.

The two young men will not only carry on the business, but also the traditions and the respect for nature that go along with it.

Silvio and his parents are natives of Angoli, and he even has a first cousin by the exact same name who owns and operates a mill that produces specially designed wood products for construction. Obviously, cousin Silvio is a good customer. During our conversation, he explained to me how the government preserves the forest. To cut trees, you must get permission from the Calabrian authorities after submitting a presentation, including the need and rationale for doing so. Silvia sees his business as a prime example of how people adapt to their surroundings and use its available resources to survive.

It is a demonstration of the peoples' character, he said. "Life here comes with resilience, because to survive we know from our history how to overcome negative events and the difficulties of life. We have the ability to be friendly and welcoming to others because of our strong sense of belonging to this area and to our traditions," Silvio concluded.

In Search of Cheese and Produce Production

There is an artisan produced local cheese *(fromaggio)* sold at the Angoli market which I cannot get enough of. It comes in a small wheel weighing about one pound; it is soft, creamy and has a medium sharpness. It slices easily like a stick of butter and melts in your mouth barely having to chew it.

One day my friend Gaetch Lucia and I set out in my car to find the cheese maker named Pasquale who lives in Amato, a comune village not too distant from Angoli. We roamed the mountains around Amato on one lane horrible roads, and finally discovered, after several inquiries, Pasquale lives in the town-center but his cheese production is in a different location. After speaking with him on the phone, it was decided we should call him the following day and set up an appointment. After being in the car for two hours, we stopped for coffee in Amato and then went to another nearby village, Miglierina, to see Vincenzo Scalise, a wholesale produce grower and distributor. He already had a list of questions from me (in Italian) which I gave him after we first met at the pub in Angoli. He was not there, but I am scheduled to see him again in a few days.

It was customary in years past for families living in the clustered houses in Angoli to have a garden plot outside of town some kilometer or two away. Gaetch and his family have such a plot on about an acre of land and bordered by the plots of other families. The plots (P71) are surrounded by forest and situated on a gently sloping hill with an old stone farmhouse at the bottom. The sloping terrain is terraced into large rectangular growing areas approximately 50 by 75 yards. All the growing areas have irrigation. When Gaetch was a child, he would play there while his grandparents worked the gardens; and during the growing season, they often stayed overnight in the old house. Today, only a few of the terraces are used.

The Soil Is My Heart and Soul

The Vincenzo Scalise family live in the village of Miglierina, just a kilometer or two away from Amato.

There the entire family, consisting of Vincenzo (P72), his wife, two sons and a daughter, work at the produce growing and distribution business which stretches out over many acres in several different locations. Attached to their home is a large warehouse where the produce is sorted and crated in small wooden boxes, loaded on trucks and "taken to market." Vincenzo and his sons till the fields, plant the vegetables and pick the harvest, while his wife works in the warehouse and his daughter keeps the books and records even though she has a full-time job working for the municipality of Miglierina. Vincenzo's two brothers are also growers and their produce is sold through his distribution system.

For the surrounding area, Vincenzo is a large-scale organic farmer who strongly believes the forest, the trees and the uncontaminated air are a very important medicine for the people. For a man with no formal education, he has done very well for himself and his family. "I love and respect the unity among the people here," he proudly told me. "Here in the mountain villages the people are always welcoming." To Vincenzo, the entire mountain region is a special, pristine place, because, he says, "We breathe pure air and drink pure water."

Vincenzo's business is a major supplier to the huge wholesale produce market ("agroalimentare") in Catanzaro, the capital city of Calabria. He also supplies some of the smaller markets in the mountains; but how fortunate the city dwellers are for the Scalise family labors in Miglierina.

Artisan Cheese Supreme

Amato is a comune like Serrastretta, and quite close to Angoli. It has a beautiful town center and *piazza* with a unique architectural appeal fitting for a movie set. If you drive to the far edge of town, opposite the direction from which you entered Amato, you come to a hilltop where civilization seems to end. You are at the beginning of a steep lane just wide enough for one vehicle, and you look out at the expanse of the horizon with views of the coast line and the sea some 25 miles away. The lane is the entrance to the property and home of Pasquale Mazza, the cheese maker. After navigating the rutted terrain, you arrive on a long, narrow peninsula of land, which falls off on both sides into a deep brush filled canyon. The peninsula is about 50 feet wide and accommodates Pasquale's house and out buildings. When I got out of my car, I saw no livestock around, but could hear the clanging of cow bells.

A young boy came out of the house, so I asked for Pasquale (P73) and the boy pointed toward the out buildings. Within a minute, Pasquale approached me, and our conversation began with my giving him a list of written questions in Italian. He understood fully and said he would return his responses to Rosetta at the Angoli market on his next delivery. Even though he made regular deliveries to the market, it took me two more visits and about three weeks trying to receive his responses. I feel he was intimidated by the situation to respond in writing probably because he is not comfortable with his Italian language skills in written form. In the end, I never did get any answers to my written questions, but I did get to know him and meet his livestock; and I still enjoy his cheese.

The people featured in this chapter are wedded to the soil; in a relationship with it that runs far deeper than their stained hands and the dirt under their fingernails. Surely, they have earned the trust and respect of Catone, the philosopher and politician of the early Roman Empire, who did not trust a person without stained and dirty hands for they were not in touch with the soil.

CHAPTER XI

The Wisdom Of Age – living In A Bubble

(La Saggezza Dell'eta –Vivendo In Una Bolla)

*"When I thought I was learning to live,
I was also learning to die"*
— Leonardo da Vinci

The populations of Serrastretta and its villages are aging with increasing pace as more of the young are choosing to leave for higher education and jobs. According to the latest available statistics, a majority of Angoli's residents are over 50 years of age; only about 20 percent of the village population is under 20 years of age. There are many seniors to engage in conversation as they gather in the afternoon under the huge tree fronting the café and market to gossip, reminisce, or play cards. The card games they play are completely foreign to me, and do not use the traditional deck of 52 cards with clubs, diamonds, hearts and spades. Some of the games they play are *"briscola," "tresette"* and *"scopa."*

What you do not hear is complaining about physical ailments. I have yet to witness a funeral in Angoli, although I am sure I will; and the words used to commemorate the life of the deceased should provide great insight on the character of the person and the role of resilience in their life. There is little need in the Calabrian mountain villages for assisted living or nursing home facilities; families always take care of their own. A local doctor kindly took the time to explain the Italian health care system and its program of "socialized medicine." Because of it, there is no large market for health insurance coverage. Primary care from internists is free to everyone, as are necessary surgical procedures. However, certain types of care the patient must pay for, such as visits to specialists. Some other fees do apply, but they do not seem to be burdensome. I have heard no one complain about the system or health care in general.

One Sunday after mass, I met Irene Mazzei and following some casual conversation she invited me to her home for coffee with her family at 3:00pm that afternoon. She lives in *Crichi Soprano,* in one of the 10 or so clustered houses; and I made the climb on foot totally out of breath when I reached the first house. I stopped to rest clinging onto whatever I could grab. Not knowing which house was Irene's, I took a few minutes to catch my breath when luckily a young man who spoke English came to my assistance and escorted me to her front door. It was there that I met her grandfather, Giuseppe Mazzei, a spry, very short 92-year-old with a full head of white hair making him look younger than his years. After meeting the rest of her family, we all sat around the dining room table; and the drinking began.

Surprisingly, we started with wine and not coffee, as the old man kept refilling my glass. Little did I know he has a village-wide reputation for his ability to consume large amounts of fortified beverages. Our wine was followed by coffee with liqueur, then shots of scotch, then more wine. I had to keep covering my glass with my hand, all the time worrying about how I would walk back down the steep hill.

The more the senior Mazzei drank, the louder he spoke, and every so often, he would pound on his chest and exclaim, *"Vivro fino a cento!"* ("I will live until 100!"). Quite possibly, he is defying da Vinci's philosophy of life and death.

Luckily, Irene drove me back down the hill to the *"piazza"* of San Giuseppi in the center of Angoli.

On another beautiful summer day, late in the morning, I walked to the café and market *"piazza"* which was full of residents and seasonal visitors, renewing old friendships and chatting with relatives. I mingled among the small crowd and engaged in several conversations. One of the visitors I spoke to, a relative from the north of Italy, expressed a strongly held opinion of life in Calabria, Serrastretta and Angoli, putting it in these words, and I paraphrase: The people here are so close to their own situation, they do not fully understand who they are, the unique significance of their lives and the gifts they have. They are not unappreciative of anything, but they cannot see the forest for the trees. Expressed in Italian, *"Non possono vedere la foresta per gli alberi."*

One of the very last research exercises I tackled was assembling all the residents of Angoli, 75 or older, by inviting them to the pub for food and drink to engage them in a group discussion on resilience and its impact on their lives and the lives of their family members. Hopefully, they would feed off one another, and one story would lead to another. But to my great surprise, the event did not turn out that way at all. By some measure, one might consider it a total failure. Just when I thought I had the village of Angoli and its residents figured out, I was again surprised at how I misjudged a situation. On my 215th day in Calabria, I anticipated this gathering of senior citizens would produce a wealth of information on resilience for this chapter. It did not, but I learned a great deal more than I expected; and what I learned is relevant to my understanding of the cultural climate that exists here.

Before the event was to begin at 5:00pm, I was charged up to get underway, but the employees of the pub did not arrive until 5:30pm, which is not too unusual in Calabrian time. While I was waiting between 5:00pm and 5:30pm, Carmelo Mazzei's father, Paulo, kept parading up and down the street in front of the pub out of curiosity, not to attend the event. Several times he came up to me to tell me in Italian I did not understand the people here because I am an American, unlike him who is a real Italian. I responded by agreeing with him, pointing to the ground where Americans are, then pointing to the sky where Italians are. He understood and seemed to appreciate my comment. Then he made a gesture intimating I think I can get by here just by throwing my money around. If he only knew how little I have. Paulo is by no means typical of the older generation in Angoli, but his attitude serves to suggest to me that the people here have a comfort zone inside their cocoon, and as they grow older, they live in a bubble. They can see out, but do not venture there; others can see in, but are welcome only up to a point.

During the 30 minutes I was waiting for the pub to open, I kept telling myself not to get frustrated because everything that happens has a reason and helps me better understand the people's psyche. Then I wondered if I have been here too long, and was now generally thought of as an intruder; another question I will never have answered. If I am inside the bubble, it is a place I do not want to stay. My observations of the older men here is based on watching most of them do nothing. Only a very few seem to keep themselves busy with hobbies, crafts or outdoor activities. It is almost as if they have lost their resilience after spending most of their life at hard work and supporting a family. Is the underlying question here this: Has resilience come full circle? I questioned four of the seniors who said they would attend but did not, and their response was to shrug it off as if to suggest it interrupted their routine. One of them, Gaetano Lucia (P74) is one of three men with the same name in this village of 300 people. He lives in *nuovo* Angoli, and every day at about 3:00pm he walks down to the market for conversation, staying approximately two hours; and then goes back up the hill to his home, covering the one kilometer distance with the help of his cane. Routines with little or nothing to do are common inside the bubble; and this brings to mind a verse I wrote two years ago titled "Changing Routines."

CHANGING ROUTINES

There are times when the mind is
Filled with a void, an emptiness; and
You chide yourself for your impatience,
When the words just don't seem to flow.
Like waiting for rain so the creeks don't dry;
No lightning strikes, as hard as you try.

Routines are too much of what they are;
Cherished, they create their own boredom.
Casting their spell, not to be broken;
While waiting to see if it might pass, but
The only thing generated is fear of the dark.
The power is out while waiting for a spark.

Finding the strength to begin anew;
Hesitation grows the longer one waits.
It stays hidden so very late in the cycle.
Time is now the enemy you once loved;
Why exchange new routines for the old?
Life goes on, doubt is a beautiful thing!

The event finally got underway at 6:00pm, with only three guests in attendance, all women. I had expected between 10 and 15 would be there, based on handing out flyers and my discussions with people in advance. Even a few who said they would attend did not come. The three ladies were Gaetch's mother, Irenea Mascaro, and Assunta Scalise and her sister Filomena. They made themselves comfortable together at a booth even though it was very cold in the pub. After they enjoyed a drink and while their food was being prepared, Assunta took it upon herself to drive home for a bag of fuel (pellets) for the pellet stove. She returned in 10 minutes and we got the fire going. After they ate, Gaetch and I sat down with them for a discussion. Women never seem to lose their resilience because they are always doing household chores and keeping the family ties together. One gets the impression they have no real concept of resilience because it has been such a part of their lives, it defines them with no second thought. They are the strength that binds. It is their children and grandchildren who will guarantee the survival of local traditions, and the villages themselves. Regardless of whether the young people stay or move elsewhere, if these women did a good job, survival is assured; this I am confident of.

As the event was fully underway, Paulo Mazzei walked by again. I went outside, took him by the arm, and invited him in for a drink. He entered, but did not stay, as I am sure he felt embarrassed. He left and went back to his bubble.

The seniors of Angoli fight every day of their lives to stay alive and enjoy the celebration. They, more than anyone, know best how fortunate they are and the values they possess, values that no one can take away or alter. They *"vivi la vita,"* enjoying every moment because of their deep devotion to family, faith and nature. And after their life ends, they are honored and revered for years to come (P75).

CHAPTER XII

Discovering The Unknown – Closer To My Roots

(Alla Scoperta Dell'Ignoto - Piu Vicino Alle Mie Radici)

"I am an Italian American. My roots are deep in ancient soil, drenched by the Mediterranean sun and watered by pure streams from snow-capped mountains. I am enriched by thousands of years of culture. My hands are those of the mason, the artist, the man of soil. My thoughts have been recorded in the annals of Rome, the poetry of Virgil, the creations of Dante, and the philosophy of Benedetto Croce. I am an Italian American, and from my ancient world I first spanned the seas to the New World – I am Christoforo Columbo. I am Giovanni Caboto, known in American history as John Cabot, discoverer of the mainland of North America. I am Amerigo Vespucci, who gave my name to the new world, America. I am Enrico Tonti, first to sail on the Great Lakes in 1679, founder of the territory that became the State of Illinois, colonizer of Louisana and Arkansas. I am Filippo Mazzei, friend of Thomas Jefferson, and my thesis on the equality of man was written into the bill of rights. I am William Paca, signer of the Declaration of Independence and, yes, an Italian American. I am an Italian American. I am Colonel Francesco Virgo – I financed the Northwest expedition of George Rogers Clark and accompanied him through the lands that would become Ohio, Indiana, Wisconsin and Michigan..."

— Angelo Biachi

From Pennsylvania restauranteur J. DeFranco

The great Italians mentioned above who contributed to America's development are but just a few. The Italians of Calabria and particularly of Serrastretta demonstrated a greatness far beyond Columbus, Vespucci and the others. These honored American discoverers, or heroes, were usually sponsored by royalty or came from wealthy Italian families allowing them to venture out and explore a new world. Not so for the millions of Calabrians and other Italian immigrants who came to America between 1880 and 1920; they made the journey out of necessity to survive, thereby calling upon far greater perseverance and adaptability, the primary characteristics of resilience. And, if they had not come, America would not be what it is today.

My cousin Tim Bevevino from Warren, Pennsylvania and the son of another cousin was the first and only Bevevino family member to visit Angoli until my arrival. Warren, in northwestern Pennsylvania where the Allegheny River begins and flows south to Pittsburgh, is the hometown of Rosario Bevevino and Rosa Scalise once they arrived in America from their birthplace, Angoli. Warren is the only place they ever lived in the United States. Tim visited Angoli about five years ago for only one day, and I recall speaking to him about it prior to the 2015 Bevevino family reunion in Warren. I was also told about his visit by the local resident who escorted him around Angoli; and I doubt Tim realized his escort was a relative, Paolo Mazzei, father of Carmelo Mazzei, owner of the one café/market in Angoli.

My months in Calabria, in Serrastretta and in Angoli, have opened a completely new world to me, and have allowed me to reach a full understanding of my grand-parents, their remarkable qualities as pioneering immi-grants, as parents and as human beings. I can now speak with some authority about their resilience and its origins.

After visiting the local cemetery several times, I could not find the tombs of Rosario's adoptive parents, Brigida Scalise and Felice Mazzei, or of Rosa's parents, Angelo Antonio Scalise and Maria Teresa Lucia. There is an explanation; after about four generations have passed, the remains are removed from their concrete or marble coffins stacked on shelves in family mausole-ums. This is done because those living would not have known them, and it creates additional space for family members to follow. I was told the remains are repack-aged and stored by the family somewhere. The oldest markers I found were a few Scalise and Mazzei tombs of people born around 1850. The birth years do not match with any of the records I have, but one or the other could be incorrect.

Prior to my coming to Calabria, Bevevino family members had gathered a substantial amount of infor-mation about our genealogy. Much of it was researched from birth, baptismal, marriage and death records in Serrastretta, and some from stories handed down by my grandparents. The Scalise family can be traced back to Sicily before their arrival in Serrastretta in the late 13th century, almost 800 years ago. According to Rabbi Barbara Aiello, there are records in Sicily documenting the fact that at least one Scalise family member was burned at the stake by the Inquisition. Understandable why they and other Jewish families escaped to a then remote area of Calabria.

According to my grandfather, an orphan born of unknown parents and adopted into the Scalise family, his natural father was a *"carribinieri"* or *"poliziotto"* in Serrastretta and his natural mother was from a local family in the silk or silk worm growing trade; and after his birth, she was banished to Brazil. But, we do not know exactly who they were, yet still hoping to find the answers. If you fast-track forward 500 years, definitive records of the Scalise family genealogy starting around 1800 document the marriage of Antonio Scalise and Concetta Lucia in 1821. They had two children, Giuseppe Scalise (1822-1895) and Maria Teresa Scalise (1812-1898). Their offspring included Brigida Scalise (1844-1929) and Angelo Antonio Scalise (1856- ?). Brigida had seven children with her husband Felice Mazzei plus their adopted son Rosario Bevivino. Angelo married Maria Teresa Lucia and they had five children including my grandmother Rosa Scalise. Rosario and Rosa married in 1905 in Warren, Pennsylvania. Rosa gave birth to nine children (seven boys followed by two girls) between 1906 and 1923. Eight of their nine children produced 36 grandchildren, 91 great-grandchildren, 113 great-great-grandchildren and to date, eight great-great-great-grandchildren. Two hundred twenty-five descendants of Rosario and Rosa gathered together in Warren, September 5-6, 2015 for a family reunion.

The spelling of the family last name was mistakenly changed after Rosario arrived in the United States. Regardless, it is a blessing to know as much as we do about the Bevevino genealogy, but mysteries remain. Who were Rosario's natural parents, why was he given the name Bevivino, and why did Brigida adopt him so quickly after his birth? There are theories, based on some fact, to answer these questions. Rosario was baptized on the day of his birth by Don Natale Fabiano in Angoli's church of San Giuseppe (P76). The priest gave him the name Rosarius Alojsius Fonte (Latin, and Fonte was probably chosen because of the baptismal font). He was then transported that sane day to Serrastretta by Brigida and Maria Gigliotti, the midwife who delivered him, arriving at 9:11pm. He was placed on the wheel of the foundling home on Strada Crocicchia, a house still standing but without the wheel. In front of two witnesses, Rosario's civil birth record was written, his name was changed to Rosario Bevivino and he was given to Brigida for adoption. The following day, the civil document was registered at the Serrastretta city hall. Brigida and Rosario returned to Angoli (P77,78,79) and some days later, the baptismal record was changed by covering over his baptismal name with a piece of paper and rewriting the name Rosario Bevivino.

Possibly Rosario's natural father was a Bevivino, although the family story is told that Rosario himself said it was Bevilaqua, so it could be the witnesses made the leap from water to wine. Concerning my great grandfather being a policeman, I made several attempts to find out by inquiring at the local police station in Serrastretta and at the Caribinieri office on the southern edge of town; both turned out to be dead ends. I was told by the local police they could not research this without a year of birth and a first name to go with Bevivino or Bevilaqua. The carabinieri told me the records are in the archives in Catanzuro, the capital city of Calabria, and I would have to go there to inquire. As for Rosario's natural mother, we know even less, but it is quite possible that Brigida cared for the young woman during her pregnancy and promised to take care of her baby. Brigida obviously knew the mother very well, and she may have even worked for the family that grew silk worms in the area, quite possibly with the name Gallo or Leone because research by Rabbi Barbara Aiello suggests they were there. All of this leads to another question: why was Maria Gigliotti brought all the way from Serrastretta to deliver the baby when there were surely midwives in Angoli. It is obvious the mother's family wanted little to do with her since they banished her to Brazil for the shame she brought upon them. As I near completion of this book, Don Emmanuel is researching the Angoli church records to see if a female child with the name Gallo or Leone was baptized there during a 10 year spam between 1855 and 1865, making her approximately 18 to 20 years old when Rosario was born.

I was told by several people in Angoli that families with the Bevivino name can be found in the village of Tiriolo, 20 kilometers east of Serrastretta. On a sunny December morning after I met with Mayor Molinaro, I decided to visit Tiriolo. The drive from Serrastretta took about 20 minutes. I parked my car in the town center and went into the nearest café. It was 11:30, so I ordered a compari soda and struck up a conversation with the young woman behind the bar. When I presented my card, her eyes lit up, and with her quite good English, she told me there were many Bevivinos in Tiriolo; and her cousin is married to a Bevivino. We continued our conversation, and she recommended I have lunch at Ristorante Dua Mari up the mountain at the highest point in the town. I took her advice, telling her I would be back to meet as many Bevivinos as possible. The restaurant is combined with a small hotel and offers a spectacular panoramic view, both east and west, so the seas on both sides of the Italian peninsula are clearly visible. I had a very good lunch for a reasonable price, and spent some time in discussion with the owner and his wife, the chef. The gave me a brochure from a local company, *Bevivino Arredo Cucine,* which specializes in the fabrication and installation of gourmet kitchens. I asked them to inform as many people as possible about my visit and I would return to meet as many Bevivinos I could find.

Not two days had gone by and I returned to Tiriolo for a second visit. It was a Sunday and I went to 11:00am mass at the church in the town's piazza, Santa Maria della Grazie. After the service, I introduced myself to the pastor, Don Giovanni Marotta, and he understood some of what I was saying about my reason for being there. He then introduced me to several others, one a woman, Marisa Badolato who was fluent in English. She took great interest in my story and liked the idea I might host a reception for all Bevivinos in Tiriolo. She offered her assistance, gave me her phone number and asked that I stay in touch. We ended our visit and I returned to Angoli knowing I had made significant progress in the search to identify Rosario Bevevino's natural father. Not only are there Bevivinos in Tiriolo, but also Bevilaquas, meaning we can be certain my great grandfather was of one or the other name. I was then contacted via email by Rossana Bevivino from Tiriolo which led to a meeting with her and her family at the Gallo Café in Serrastretta.

They traced their family back to the time of Rosario Bevevino's birth and they do not believe there was a relative who was a policeman. Their ancestor alive then as a young male adult was Vincenzo Bevivino from Tiriolo who worked road construction in and around Serrastretta and Angoli. With Rossana's help, we have scheduled a reception on January 6 at Dua Mari for all Bevivinos in Tiriolo. She told me during one of our conversations that her family was motivated to meet with me because in 2014 her father received a letter my cousins Dan and Susan, and I, wrote to several Bevivinos we found in the Calabrian telephone directory. He never responded to the letter, but when I showed up in Tiriolo, he made the connection.

The reception was held as planned, and it led to new discoveries and information. The Bevivino family in Tiriolo can trace its genealogy to its beginning there when Vincenzo Bevivino arrived from another village (Filadeifia), 40 or more kilometers away. They showed me a schematic of their family tree, meaning all the Bevivinos in Tiriolo are of one family beginning with Vincenzo. The family is very close knit, and the oldest member alive is Rossana's grandmother, Rosa Critelli, the mother of Rossana's father, Oreste. All of this discovery now leads me to believe Rosario Bevevino's father was probably Vincenzo, born about 1855. He started his own family in Tiriolo with the birth of his first child, Marianna in 1889, with his wife Maria Parone, just six years after Rosario's birth (P80,81).

This makes practical, historical sense. Here was a single, young man, new to Tiriolo, who finds a job in road construction taking him 20 kilometers away from

Tiriolo which means he would not have returned there every day after work; therefore, he became known in Serrastretta and Angoli, where Rosario was born. When Brigida Scalise took Rosario to Serrastretta on June 5, 1883 to register his birth and adopt him, as the city hall records testify, the registration document was witnessed by two men who obviously knew who the father was; and they renamed him Rosario Bevivino. This act labeled Rosario as not one of their own because his father was an "out-of-towner" who impregnated one of their young women.

All of this helps to explain why Rosario would never return to Angoli, despite repeated offers by his own adult children to take him back for a visit. He knew who his natural parents were, yet his mother was sent away and his father, and possibly even the people of Angoli, shunned or ignored him. As an adopted child in a very large family in a very small village, it is easy to understand why, at age 19, he left for America. His childhood step-cousin and future wife Rosa would follow him one year later.

How is it they were able to go to America? Rosa's older sister Giuseppina was married to Giuseppe Iuliano and the couple was already in Warren, Pennsylvania. They became the sponsors for those who followed. The two families shared a house on Fourth Street in Warren, but when the families grew larger, the house was too small. Giuseppe and Rosario flipped a coin; the toss went to Rosario, and from that time on, he alone owned the house. It was the Bevevino homestead where all their nine children were born, and it remained in family hands until very recently. Rosario had previously won another contest with a Iuliano in Warren, for his wife to be, Rosa Scalise. Before her arrival in America, she was betrothed to a Iuliano in Warren. Years later, when asked by one of my cousins what happened to the betrothal, Rosario explained it this way in his accented, broken English: "When Rosa first arrived, we run to each other and are hugging and kissing, because when Rosa sees me, it is goodbye Joe." Rosa was always working, helping to tend the family gardens, baking bread or tending to her chickens, and she would never slaughter one if it was about to lay an egg. One of her brood decided to come back to life in her kitchen after she beheaded it on a tree stump behind the house, and there was blood splattered everywhere.

The other wonderful stories about Rosario and Rosa in America are many, and they are handed down from one generation to the next. I treasure my personal memories of them because as a child and young adolescent, I knew them well. I witnessed their strength, their pride in family and their resilience. Speaking of strength, Rosario was one of the most physically powerful men I have ever known. He had huge hands and could use a 16-pound sledge hammer like a carpenter's smaller version. I once met Mohammed Ali, the boxer, and when I shook his hand I remember thinking it was comparable in size to my grandfather's. An example of his power and strength comes from an incident during his 40-year career on the railroad. He was being considered for a promotion, and one of his coworkers persisted in fabricating negative stories to prevent the promotion. Rosario went to this man, took him by the neck with one hand, raised him in the air and said: "If you don't stop, I will kill you." It was a warning and a threat because to Rosario, the man was threatening his family. Another wonderful story about Rosario demonstrates his character as a Calabrian from Serrastretta. A young Iuliano man from Warren, Pennsylvania got into trouble and was imprisoned in Rhode Island; and it was Rosario who traveled there, had an audience with the state's governor and convinced him to release the young man. An example, yet again, of looking after one another.

I was invited to the home of Gaetano Lucia's mother for a three-hour, six course mid-afternoon lunch and the pasta she served was *"timpano"* which my grandmother made. It was explained to me that the dish is an Angoli original; it consists of baked spaghetti with varying ingredients like hard-boiled eggs, meatballs, sausage, salami, then covered with grated cheese and cut like wedges of cake. Other names for similar versions of this dish depending on the Calabrian locale are *"pastachina"* and *"sartu."*

The other food I recall are deep fried small sausage shaped foods made from potatoes, vegetables (usually eggplant) or meat. The Italian generic name is *"vrasciole."* A variation of that name is used for the meat version, and as a child, I remember my father calling it *"rascoli"* or something close to that. He used to spend the better part of a day on Saturday making them with help from me and my sisters. As an engineer, he even went so far as to design and fabricate an extrusion machine for the meat mixture to speed up the process.

I will never forget my grandmother's passing and the days leading up to her death. Everyone in the family knew it was only a matter of days, and we each took our turn at her bedside; and as 11-year-olds, my twin sister and I knelt by the bed as she held our hands and apologized for not being able to make us pasta any longer. The mourning at the funeral home and the funeral mass were on very hot summer days, and it was shoulder-to-shoulder standing room only in front of her open casket. Several people fainted, and several elderly Italian women, including Rosa's sister, literally tried to pull her out of the casket. The memory is eerily vivid and I still picture it in my mind.

These two remarkable Italian Americans were born and raised in a tiny village on a mountain top in central Calabria where life was harsh, where hard work was a way of life and nothing came easy. They brought their values and their love for life from Angoli di Serrastretta to Warren, Pennsylvania; and they passed this on to their children: Joseph, Angelo, William, Anthony, Frank, John, Rosina and Lorraine.

The village of Angoli is known as the "Second Office" of Serrastretta because it was the first of the villages to be settled (around 1695) once Serrastretta became overcrowded and the land suitable for agriculture too limited. Today, even though Angoli is shrinking, as is Serrastretta and its other villages, it still exudes a warmth, friendliness and family atmosphere. It truly is a place where *"Celabrazione di Vita"* (The Celebration of Life} is paramount. Because Rosario was an illegitimate child, he was denied full participation in this until he went to America. At the 2015 Bevevino Family Reunion, a tribute to him was read to the large audience. It referred to him as a "true patriarch," and concluded with these words:

"Here's to the simplest of men, yet the greatest of men. And, if you were to ask him how he achieved such greatness, he would simply look at you, smile and utter the last word to cross his lips ...'Rosa'."

Rosario Bevevino lived to be 95, and died in 1978, 25 years to the day that Rosa Scalise Bevevino passed away.

One late afternoon when I was at the restaurant/bar in Angoli, a man approached me and introduced himself as Ugo Mazzei. He spoke very little English, but I understood him to say he had a great amount of knowledge about the history of Angoli, and he would see me again the following day with his doctor who spoke English. Instead of "doctor" he meant to say "daughter." He and his daughter Wanessa came to my residence and the three of us spent two hours in conversation as he impressed upon me his pride in helping visitors to Angoli uncover information about their roots. Ugo's permanent residence is now in France, but he has a large home in Angoli where he and his family spend six months a year.

Two days later I was at his home, met the rest of his family and enjoyed a wonderful blueberry liqueur while he showed me many old photos and documents. One of the old photos showed the row of stone houses on the main street (then Via Valentino) next to the church. Birth documents of the children of Brigida Scalise and Felice Mazzei testify to the fact their children were born at No. 13 *Via Valintino,* which means Rosario Bevivino lived there and was probably born there. The old photo was taken between 1930 and 1940, and the row of old houses was demolished to widen the main street.

When the homes were no longer occupied, they were used to house community bread ovens. It could very well be that Angelo Antonio Scalise and Maria Teresa Lucia (Rosa's family) lived on *Via Crichi* or what is called *Crichi Soprano* (High Crichi), a section of homes on a hill high above the center of Angoli. At one time there were 20 or 30 homes in *Crichi Soprano.* The two are in easy walking distance, but it is a very steep climb and puts a tremendous strain on your legs. There was also a section of homes in *Crichi Sottano* or Low Crichi just below *Crichi Soprano.* Today there is a section of newer homes on the road out of town toward Serrastretta called, of course, *Nuovo Angoli.*

The thought just struck me like a bolt of lightning that when I was a young boy around my grandparents from Angoli, I was unable to appreciate what I had; and now I do. I was a witness to their resilience and their values without knowing it. It is my greatest hope to share this with descendants of Calabrians in America to help identify who they are and take comfort in the efforts of all Americans to honor their roots making the USA a stronger place for the future.

Rosario Bevevino (son of Angoli) – proud to be an Italian, proud to be an Italian American, proud to be an American Italian, and proud to be an American.

CONCLUSION
(Conclusione)

"Observe the flame of a candle and consider its beauty.
Blink your eye and look at it again.
What you see now was not there before, and
what was there before is not there now.
Who is it that rekindles the flame that is always dying?"
— Leonardo da Vinci

The quotation above by Leonardo da Vinci suggests to me that there is a conclusion to nothing; instead, there is a continuance of life that moves us forward, always burning, yet always dying. Call it nature, as Leonardo did, and those who best persevere and adapt survive the longest. Resilience personified; and those who know best how to rekindle the flame are the people of Sicily, Calabria and Serrastretta.

Possibly the greatest tribute paid Leonardo da Vinci came from a close friend and contemporary, King Francis I of France. He was reported to be at Leonardo's bedside when he died. An early da Vinci biographer said of the French monarch, "He did not believe that any other man had come into the world who had attained so great knowledge as Leonardo, and not only as sculptor, painter, and architect, far beyond that he was a profound philosopher." The biographer, Morelli, went on to say of Leonardo, "His personality projected by the inherent force of its vitality down into modern times, and so to take its due place among the intuitive influences of modern thought." Morelli concluded, "Perhaps the most richly gifted by nature among all the sons of men."

Resilience can be defined using a variety of words by different people in Calabria. Some of the words that stand out to me, all used by Calabrians in my interviews and discussions with them, include sacrifice, desire, passion, honesty, stubbornness, suffering, attitude, independent, resourceful, clever, courage, winning at life, intuition, energy, faith, and hope. They all equally apply, and none is any more important than another. A people possessing a combination of these characteristics are almost indistructable.

During my months in Calabria, I attended mass virtually every Sunday when that was not a habit of mine during many prior years. I did so to observe and participate with the people who are the subject of this book. There is one thing that has troubled me throughout my discoveries and my writing. To put it simply, it is the observation that the Catholic Church in Italy is slowly dying. It is not that the people there are losing their faith in a higher being, or even in the Holy Trinity; rather it is that the Church has so dated itself, it has allowed the faithful of today's modern world to surpass it. When one observes the practice of Catholicism in Calabria, he is thrown back in time to the days when Calabrians first went to America. You observe a Church of this higher authority wherein the clergy are the keepers of knowledge, and the faithful are spoon fed on a need to know basis. As supporting evidence of this: in most older churches in Italy, there is a pulpit box or balcony situated at the front of the church perched half way up to the ceiling from where homilies were given. Is any more evidence needed to suggest "talking down?" In today's more modern Catholic Church, as witnessed in the United States, the people take a much more active, leadership role resulting in a much greater sense of community and participation. I may be wrong in my assessment, but I fear that if things do not change, death will surely come; and all that remains will be the Vatican in Rome. I have believed for most of my adult life that the only thing wrong with the Catholic religion is the institution of the Catholic Church, an institution made by man. Its salvation is to serve the many, not the few.

However, the practice of Catholicism in Italy suffers from a stark contradiction, and the opposite view might suggest that in this contradiction there is a salvation. Most who I spoke with have a mistrust and a dislike for the institution of the Catholic Church, but they love and trust in their religion and their faith. This becomes apparent when you witness the festival of a beloved patron saint; no institution, no Vatican, no pope, cardinal, bishop, or priest can take this away from them. Unlike American Catholics, this faith and trust in God and their patron is passed on to them by the bond of strong family values. The ultimate irony of this decline in worship is the fact that new and bigger churches are being constructed, such as in the villages of Accaria and Cancello. Maybe, just maybe, their community has and will continue to thrive in the family, at least for as long as it stays closely connected, unlike in America. If man persists in the denial of his past through some misguided judgement or a disrespect for his own origins, there is little hope for the future. Man is nature in its highest form, and he has been blessed with gifts possessed by no other creatures. Our ability to reason and make choices bears a serious responsibility, a responsibility to respect not only others, but also ourselves and from where it is we came. Self-destruction is a choice, one that Calabrians and the people of Serrastretta will never make.

Among Italian Americans, we often brag with some bravado about our historical contributions to America. It goes like this: We discovered it, we named it, and we built it. True, there is some exaggeration in those words, but Columbus and Vespucci were real life Italians, and if five million Calabrians had not gone to the United States between 1880 and 1920, would our country be the same today? The skills they brought with them, their faith and the belief in family, and most of all their work ethic, has contributed enormously to defining our country.

In the Introduction at the beginning of the book, I raised several questions about resilience. What is it? Where does it come from? Is it inbred and self-sustaining? Can it be lost and rediscovered? Was the emigration of Europeans to America in the late 19th and early 20th centuries a prime example of resilience?

Most simply stated, resilience is the ability to recover from or adjust easily to misfortune or change. It is born of centuries old hardships, and literally thousands of years of change, experienced by the people who were and are today Sicilians and Calabrians. Whether resilience is genetically inbred must be left to science, but surely it is self-sustaining; time has proven that to be a fact. My grandparents, Rosario Bevevino and Rosa Scalise were living proof of resilience. There are few places on this earth like Serrastretta where families have carried on their names and traditions so long. Those names (Bruni, Fazio, Mancuso, Scalise and Talarico) and their traditions long preceded the exodus of those five Jewish families who made their way to Calabria from Sicily almost 800 years ago.

Who would have ever thought this book would turn out to be a love story?

As I near completion of it, I have been given the rare opportunity to work with two local men on the design and construction of a permanent monument to San Giuseppe in the *piazza* fronting the church in Angoli. Local artist Dino Iuliano and iron worker, *"officina del ferro"* Fabio Lucia and I will collaborate on the project. Dino will carve the statue of San Giuseppe and Christ in relief on stone, Fabio will fabricate the decorative iron housing and roof, and I will paint it. In so doing, I will leave my mark and the Bevevino name in the birthplace of my grandparents; and when our work is done, I will probably spend the rest of my days in Angoli di Serrastretta.

Could it be that in man's current pursuit of *"la dolce vita,"* the constant pursuit of wealth, pleasure, physical comforts and the misuse of technology, he hastens his own self-destruction even though the celebration of life is already his to behold? After all my observation and discovery, I am overwhelmed by the thought if Leonardo da Vinci were alive today, he would tell us this: "Yes, the flame is always dying, but it will never go out."

"Viva Famiglia, Viva Fede, Viva Natura, Viva Resilienza!"

PHOTO GALLERY
(Photography by the author)

(PI) **Good friend and guardian angel Sonia Bellezza**

(P2) **Monastero San Benedetto**

(P3) **Exterior view of Don Gigi's house (villa)**

(P4) **Front door of Don Gigi's house – keystone dated 1667**

(P5) **The 22-seat dining table at Don Gigi's house**

(P6) **The home of Sabrina Mazzei and Massimo Iuliano in Angoli**

(P7) **San Teodoro, the 1000-year-old Norman fortress ruin in Nicastro, on the northeastern edge of Lamezia Terme**

(P8) **One of the many roadside waterfalls
along the mountain roadways**

(P9) **A cheese makers sheep coming home for milking**

(P10) **Entering Serrastretta – Citta della Sedia**

(P11) **Main street, Serrastretta**

189

(P12) **Main doors of Serrastretta's church**

(P13) **Marking the dedication and construction of Serrastretta's church**

(P14) **Roadside shrines, some of many**

(P15) **A typical front door of an old,
still occupied house in Angoli**

(P16) **The three white crosses of Angoli at the edge of town**

(P17) **A view of Crichi Soprano in Angoli**

(P18) **Children painting the steps for the Angoli festival of San Giuseppe**

(P19) **The finished painted steps**

(P20) **Summer festival of San Giuseppe in Angoli**

(P21) **Another summer festival scene in Angoli**

(P22) **The midnight Christmas bonfire in Angoli**

(P23) **The local soccer team celebrating at the Angoli pub after a game**

(P24) **Presentation of the Chestnut Festival cheesecake in Angoli**

(P25) **Baking bread at home in Migliuso**

(P26) **Simone Lucia of Café Sunset is enjoying a caffee
at the café in Migliuso**

(P27) **Alessio Cianfilone and his father at their Migliuso market**

(P28) **Gabriella Scicchitano and Rosario Gallo
at the café in Accaria**

(P29) **Don Gigi working at home**

(P30) **Rabbi Barbara Aiello at her Serrastretta synagogue**

(P31) **Serrastretta Mayor Felice Molinaro at the Angoli summer festival**

**(P32) Maria DeSantis and Miriam Mascaro
working at the pub in Angoli**

(P33) **Elisabetta Fazio at work in the Puento market, Serrastretta**

(P34) **The wedding of Alessia Della Porta and
Cristian Iuliano in Angoli**

(P35) **Red-headed Danile Scalise at the pub in Angoli**

(P36) **Rossana Bevivino from Tiriolo**

(P37) **Luca Fragale from Accaria**

(P38) Sabrina Mazzei with her mother and her
husband Massimo Iuliano

(P39) **Rita Gallo at her Gallo Pasticceria in Serrastretta**

(P40) **Rosetta Bruni at the market/café in Angoli**

(P41) **Gaetano (Gaetch) Lucia preparing for karaoke night at the pub in Angoli**

(P42) **Gaetch behind the pub bar**

(P43) **Antonio Molinaro at his consulting/accounting office in Serrastretta**

(P44) **Francesco Gallo and Giovanni Marrone in the jewelry store workshop**

(P45) **Adriano Mazza, Serrastretta's butcher**

(P46) **Fabio Lucia in front of his foundry
with a custom table base**

(P47) **Marco Molinaro in his restaurant kitchen at E Torre**

(P48) **Pino Palletta in his showroom**

(P49) **Daniela Bilardi, neighbor and friend of Sonia Bellezza**

(P50) **Angelo Falvo, Raffele Cortese and Luca Ferrese
at the Falvo Café, Lamezia**

(P51) **The staff at the Falvo Café, Eugenio Falvo with Melinda and Paola**

(P52) **Roberta Piro working at Dorelanbed, Lamezia**

(P53) **The Duomo di Messina**

(P54) **University of Messina law students Victerio Silvestri
and Alessandro Barbera**

(P55) **Italian national police officer Vincenzo Sodano**

(P56) **Danieli Trunfio on the train from Reggio Calabria to Lamezia Terme**

(P57) **Professor Mario Gallo in his home office**

(P58) **Luigi Anania at the school in Angoli where he teaches**

(P59) **Retired language teacher Gaetano Mazzei
in front of his Angoli home**

(P60) **Cardiologist Dr. Gaspare Mancuso studying
his interview questions**

(P61) **Professor Enrico Mascaro at home working
with Rabbi Barbara Aiello**

(P62) **Don Antonio Costantino at work in his Serrastretta church**

(P63) **Don Isaac Assogbavi baptizing a new born in Angoli**

(P64) **Don Emmanuel Akuma Okoto in front of San Giuseppe's alter in Angoli**

(P65) **Don Giovanni Morotta at his Tiriolo church**

(P66) **Sister Micheline Ngonge Limolo assisting in Angoli**

(P67) **Roberto Talarico, and his team, at slaughter**

(P68) **Caterina Fiorentino making pomodoro sauce for winter**

(P69) **Delfino di Maruca and son Mattia
in front of their restaurant**

(P70) **Silvio Mascaro with one of his loaded logging trucks**

(P71) **The half abandoned farm (garden)
of the Gaetano Lucia family**

(P72) **Vincenzo Scalise, the commercial produce grower**

(P73) **Pasquale Mazza, and son, the cheese maker**

(P74) **Gaetano Lucia, the oldest of three with
the same name in Angoli**

(P75) **The cemetery serving Angoli, Migliuso and Cancello**

(P76) **The church of San Giuseppe in Angoli where Rosario Bevevino and Rosa Scalise were baptized**

(P77) **The home, just to the left of the church, of Brigida Scalise and Felice Mazzei, the adoptive parents of Rosario Bevevino**

(P78) **The location today of Rosario Bevevino's birthplace (directly in front of the right hand pink garage door)**

(P79) **The tiny stone house in Angoli where Brigida Scalise spent her last days**

(P80) **Members of today's Bevivino family from Tiriolo**

(P81) **The grandchildren of Vincenzo Bevivino
(Rosario Bevevino's half-brother and half-sisters)**

APPENDIX

(Appendice)

Map of Italy

Map of Calabria

Portrait of Leonardo da Vinci

Portrait of Rosario Bevevino

Who Was Dalida?

Verses (written by the author in contemplation
of writing *Resilience*)
> *We Are Our Past*
> *Reaching For The Light*
> *A Reach Too Far*
> *An Issue Of Trust*
> *The Next Step*
> *The Art Of Living*
> *Yes, I Can. Yes, I Can*

Maps reprinted from Karen Haid's CALABRIA, The Other Italy, published by Mill City Press, Minneapolis, 2015

**The author's painting of Leonardo de Vinci
with his father in the background**

**The author's painting of his grandfather
Rosario Bevevino at age 92**

WHO WAS DALIDA?

One of the most revered citizens of Serrastretta is an
entertainer/celebrity, a native whose name is
Iolanda Cristina Gigliotti.
Everywhere you go in Serrastretta you see her image,
painted on posters, store front slidedown security
doors, and engraved on stone plaquards. There is even
an outdoor amphitheater named in her honor, and
she has her own musem located behind the municipal
building. I sought to discover the reason for her fame
and popularity, so I reached out to Angelo Aiello, secretary of the *Associazione Culturale Dalida*, and sat
down with him for an interview. I had very few facts
before meeting with the secretary, but I did know she
was a nationally popular singer in the 1960's, 1970's
and 1980's; and I wanted to know more. After all, there
must be a great story behind someone with such notoriety. The story is fascinating. Dalida came from a family with great musical talent. Her father was a violinist
who spent much of his career living in Cairo, Egypt and
playing for the symphony orchestra there, although
his family home is Serrastretta. Dalida was born and
raised in Cairo where she was musically trained and
began her career, but she spent most of her adult life
in Paris where her career on stage and in films flour-
ished. She won the Miss Egypt beauty contest in 1954.
Between 1960 and 1980, she achieved fame throughout
all of Europe, selling more that 140 million albums and
singles. I put the question to Angelo and his associate
Nunzia Fazio, the museum cureator, who Dalida might

compare to in the United States. The name Barbara Streisand came immediately to mind, and we all three agreed. Unfortunately, for her family and fans, her life came to a sudden end at age 54
from an overdose of sleeping pills.

Angelo Aiello and his associate at the Dalida museum

WE ARE OUR PAST

What fools some men are thinking
History can somehow be altered
To suit our present circumstance.
I write these words on Columbus Day
To salute from where it is he came.
And now we face little, fearful men
Thinking their wisdom can sweep him away.
Ownership is ours, our history's been cast.

Others went forth from the Renaissance;
Their discoveries, like his, bear us no scars.
As badges of honor, we hold them dear.
What is it these men have so to fear?
Hollow attempts to change our history
Serve only to prove their insecurity;
Not accepting the identity of who we are,
And believing their own echo will be heard.

We are benefactors of many nameless men;
Even the greatest are seldom recalled.
Far beyond Vespucci, Caboto and Tonti;
There are others not so immortalized.
Enriching gifts of Mazzei, Paca and Virgo;

They are gone, yet here, their gifts survive.
Why rush to throw them all aside
By actions, the echo of small-minded men?

These gifts are ours, defining who we are.
To say they are not so, to reject them

Speaks loudly to the crisis of our identity.
Fools are those who seek vain perfection
By vailed attempts to put history on trial.
Surely it is impossible to better ourselves
Weighed down in a state of denial.
Celebrate our past, it is who we are.

This discourse causes one to wonder
If the day will come when others from
Our more recent past will be discarded
In the refuse of too many little men?

REACHING FOR THE LIGHT

*This verse is dedicated to Dr. David Orr, a professor
at Cornell University and poetry critic at the* New
York Times. *He is the author of the book "The Road
Not Taken," an analysis of the Robert Frost poem by
the same name. Dr. Orr's book provides the best
examination of the Frost poem, and of Frost himself.
His insights were extremely meaningful in helping
me write the following words. The writings of
David Orr and Robert Frost will remain with me on
the roads I have yet to travel. As both have said,
"And that has made all the difference."*

I am so drawn to those simpler times past,
And from where it is my family came;
Those times and places so easy to voice.
To be there, no doubt, it is my choice;
A rash decision, and a bit insane.
Thoughts impractical, but they yet remain.
To think of achieving such a reverse;
Do I dare toy with an impending curse?

There is this need to live in the past,
To honor it, how it forever lasts.
Embark I must into an unknown.
Without the fear of second guessing
My desires, my motivation as a blessing.
Now to undertake it, as best I can.
To observe, to learn, and to understand,
To keep the light burning as it began.

There is a bright light in what I must do;
Others have made such journeys before.
In ages past, from many distant shores.
The courage called upon greater than mine.
Alone at the edge of the "yellow wood"
In the hope that I will be understood;
For the road that I choose will be my last.

What a better teacher than history,
To be its witness, live its mysteries.
Reaching back to a better time and place,
To study life at a much slower pace.
The magic in all its simplicity,
Greatness I can then even touch and see.
I might tire of this chosen road,
But treasure the learning I did unfold.

THE NEXT STEP

The time is short with so much left undone,
Then to leave your print upon the earth
And prove that life has had some worth.
Where to begin to find this resting place?
Possibly a place we have already been,
Forever searching to find a way back.

No beginning for something already begun;
Void of repetition, the past is in stone.
Dreams in darkness can be filled with lies;
Upon mid-day fantasies you can't rely.
The beginning is over, life carries us
To new horizons, places still unknown.

Like ages long past,
Your footprint is cast;
Imprint the next step.
This challenge, this test,
It could be your best.
Then it's time to rest

THE ART OF LIVING

To be filled with life, its precious gifts;
Then leave your mark upon the earth.
Do not stay, said Dante, beneath the quilt,
And waste away your source of worth.
As if smoke in the air, you drift away,
Vanish like foam upon water.

Relentless, random curiosity,
Waking hours in observation
Of all that surrounds your every moment.
Your senses ignite creation.
It is then, at those moments, only then
A mark is made that you can see.

Things confusing fire the mind to greatness,
Arousing its inventiveness.
What's impossible for others to see,
Forever yours, and only yours.
Standing face to face with your own fame,
You see clearly your reflection.

AN ISSUE OF TRUST

Often I examine the issue of trust.
Can we place it in a changing world,
This "progress" to invent intelligence?
And what are the costs of these creations
If they so weaken our humanity?
Distrust of others is our destiny.

Hungering for an answer to this question;
My search, unsatisfied, just beginning.
Clues can be found searching in the past;
Many are hidden by the obvious.
Some so simple they escape recognition.
So blinded by many worn traditions.

Da Vinci's genius provides us a clue,
Yet his is a gift possessed by so few.
His genius was thirst and observation,
Not his inventions or masterpieces.
Relentless, random curiosity,
Desiring knowledge rather than to be.

Leonardo's eyes trusted in Nature,
More than lettered men, their authority,
To quench his insatiable thirst to know.

"Nature's gifts are simple and direct,
Nothing is lacking or superfluous."
Choose to emulate him with full respect.

"YES, I CAN. YES, I CAN."

There was a young man coming from far, far away
To build a new life, how he fought, but he stayed.
He married his love of many years past,
And started a dynasty guaranteed to last.

The stories are told of this powerful man
Because he believed "Yes, I can. Yes, I can."

He provided a bounty from little to start
To nurture his offspring with hands and with heart.
Steadfast with resolve, he worked and he toiled,
Bearing fruits from the passion he had for the soil.

His life became legend, this powerful man
Because he believed "Yes, I can. Yes, I can."

His family abounds, everywhere, every place;
No match for his life, or the challenge he faced.
Who was this patriarch, this man with no name?
It matters too little, for he never sought fame.

The stories are told of this powerful man
Because he believed "Yes, I can. Yes, I can."

We recall him most fondly, this simplest of men;
And wonder in awe how it all began.
Yes, a simple man, yet the greatest of men;
What a joy it would be to be with him again.

His life became legend, this powerful man
Because he believed "Yes, I can. Yes, I can."

Many of us have sprung from his vine;
Raise a glass to him, as we all drink wine.
The stories live on about this legend, this man.
Because he believed "Yes, I can. Yes, I can."

BIBLIOGRAPHY/ REFERENCES

(Bibliografia E Riferimenti)

Aiello, Rabbi Barbara. *THE JEWS OF SICILY AND CALABRIA, The Italian Anusim That Nobody Knows.* 2011. Barbara Aiello. Serrastretta, Italy

Benjamin, Sandra. *SICILY, Three Thousand Years Of Human History.* Steerforth Press. Hanover, NH

Caputo, Michael. *THE COIN FROM CALABRIA.* 2012. Michael Caputo. Canada

Caputo, Michael. *UNDER A LION SUN.* 2015. Michael Caputo. Canada

Chiarella, Peter. *CALABRIAN TALES.* 2012. Regent Press. Oakland, CA

Comune di Serrastretta. *GUIDA DI SERRASTRETTA, Storia, Arte, Cultura e Tradizioni.* 2012. Comune di Serrastretta, Italy

Douglas, Norman. *OLD CALABRIA.* 2015. Jefferson Publication. San Bernadino, CA

Gallo, Mario. *SERRASTRETTA, Fonti Storiche Di Una Comunita Operosa.* 2017. Firenze

Haid, Karen. *CALABRIA, THE OTHER ITALY.* 2015. Mill City Press. Minneapolis

Isaacson, Walter. *LEONARDO DA VINCI.* 2017. Simon & Schuster. New York

Isaacson, Walter. *"The Making Of Genius."* Vol. 190 No. 22-23, 2017 Time Magazine. New York

Kemp, Martin. *LEONARDO.* 2004. Oxford University Press. Oxford, UK

Mendola, Louis and Alio, Jacqueline. *THE PEOPLE OF SICILY, A Multicultural Legecy.* 2013. Trinacria Editions. New York

Nicholl, Charles. *LEONARDO DA VINCI, Flights Of The Mind.* 2004. Penguin Books Ltd. London

Villella, Vincenzo. *GIUDECCHE DI CALABRIA.* 2014. Editoriale Progetto 2000. Cosenza, Italy

Wasserman, Jack. *LEONARDO DA VINCI.* 2003. Harry N. Abrams, Inc. New York

ACKNOWLEGMENTS
(Riconoscimenti)

To my two heroes, only one of which I had the privilege to know personally: my father Angelo J. Bevevino and Leonardo da Vinci.

To Suzy Shultz Bevevino, whose patience and technical assistance with this project was at times painful, but always appreciated and fruitful for both of us.

To my son Loren and daughter Angela who showed great understanding for my creative pursuits.

To my twin sister Christie whose encouragement and searching questions as a "devil's advocate" always made me dig deeper for the truth.

To my dearest friend and guardian angel in Calabria, Sonia Bellezza, (il mio angelo custode) whose guiding hand was always there for me.

To Sabrina Mazzei Iuliano and Massimo Iuliano, Gaetano (Gaetch) Lucia and Carmelo Mazzei and Rosetta Bruni Mazzei whose support and friendship welcomed me into the Angoli family.

To Andrea Caruso and Gianfranco Maruca for thier invaluable translation assistance.

To my best friend and cousin Joe Bevevino who acknowledges and supports my passions without fully understanding, judging or questioning them.

To all the descendants of Rosario and Rosa Scalise Bevevino, especially Dan and Susan Bevevino, Linda Bevevino Ditka.

Also, thanks to the following individuals who believed enough in this project to order advance copies, both in the USA and Italy, thus allowing the book's publication and release to occur in a timely manner:

Frank Bevevino, Bill Bevevino, John Bevevino, Dan/Susan Bevevino, Jim Bevevino, Ross Bevevino, Christine Rexroat, Elaine Trevey, Loren Bevevino, Angela Christine Bevevino, Cindy Weakland, Larry Bevevino, Linda Ditka, Joe Bevevino; Gaetano Lucia, Antonio Molinaro, Sabrina Mazzei/Massimo Iuliano, Assunta Scalise, Francesco Gallo.

ABOUT THE AUTHOR

Chris Bevevino is a native of western Pennsylvania, raised in Butler County, about 40 miles north of Pittsburgh. He graduated high school at Saint Vincent Prep School in Latrobe, Pennsylvania, then earned his BA degree from John Carroll University in Cleveland, Ohio in 1964. He continued his education at American University in Washington, DC where he received his MA degree in Communications. His professional career was spent in Washington over 35 years in various management positions for trade and professional non-profit associations. Between 1983 and 1998, he was president and CEO of the international trade association for the business forms and systems industry. During that period, the association grew to over 850 member companies worldwide and had a European office in Berne, Switzerland. He also served on the board of the American Society of Association Executives and was chairman of its International Committee. During retirement, he has owned and managed an art gallery and custom framing business, and now pursues his writing and painting.

Phone: (619) 316-9546 (Whatsapp)
Email: crdrinkwine@outlook.com

CPSIA information can be obtained
at www.ICGtesting.com
Printed in the USA
BVHW091043270619

552119BV00025B/2089/P